PENGUIN BOOKS

KISS HOLLYWOOD GOODBYE

Anita Loos was born in 1893 and educated in San Diego, California. She was a scenario writer with D. W. Griffith for five years, with Douglas Fairbanks for three years and Constance Talmadge for two years. She wrote *Gentlemen Prefer Blondes* in 1925, the screenplay for it (in collaboration with John Emerson) in 1928, and she also adapted it for the stage as a comedy and as a musical. Since then she has adapted several of her novels, plus two by Colette, for the stage. Her publications include the novels *But Gentlemen Marry Brunettes* (with John Emerson), *A Mouse Is Born*, *No Mother to Guide Her* and the autobiography, *A Girl Like I*. In addition, Anita Loos has written the screenplay of numerous films (listed at the back of this book), which include *Red-Headed Woman*, *Blossoms in the Dust*, *I Married an Angel* and *The Pirate*.

ANITA LOOS

Kiss Hollywood Goodbye

PENGUIN BOOKS

Penguin Books Ltd, Harmondsworth, Middlesex, England
Penguin Books, 625 Madison Avenue, New York, New York 10022, U.S.A.
Penguin Books Australia Ltd, Ringwood, Victoria, Australia
Penguin Books Canada Ltd, 2801 John Street, Markham, Ontario, Canada L3R 1B4
Penguin Books (N.Z.) Ltd, 182-190 Wairau Road, Auckland 10, New Zealand

—

First published in the U.S.A. 1974
First published in Great Britain by W. H. Allen & Co Ltd 1974
Published in Penguin Books 1979

—

Copyright © Anita Loos, 1974
All rights reserved

—

Made and printed in Great Britain
by C. Nicholls & Company Ltd
Set in Linotype Juliana

I am indebted to Mr Robert Reinhart for the time and care he gave to the
preparation of the list of my screenplays beginning on page 205 – Anita Loos

Acknowledgement is made to the following for permission to quote material:
William Empson, for 'Reflection from Anita Loos' from Collected Poems.'
Reprinted by permission of the author.
Harper & Row, Publishers, Mrs Laura Huxley, Grover Smith, and Chatto &
Windus, for excerpts from The Letters of Aldous Huxley, edited by Grover Smith.
Music Sales Corp, for 'I Love What I'm Doing' by Leo Robin and Jule Styne,
from the Musical Production Gentlemen Prefer Blondes.
Copyright © Consolidated Music Publishers, Div. of Music Sales Corporation,
1949. All rights reserved. Used by permission.
Pansy Schenck, for the poem by Rudolf Friml.
The Viking Press, Inc., for an excerpt from Crazy Sundays by Aaron Latham.
Copyright © 1971 by John Aaron Latham.

For Henry Sell

Contents

I

Footprints on the Ceiling

IN my youth I never kept a diary, feeling that a girl who could sell her words for money had other fish to fry. But back in 1927 I began to save my old datebooks, which have accumulated until they now fill two wide bookshelves.

Looking them over recently, it struck me that those datebooks are more truthful than any diaries, for, as time rolled on, items which once seemed insignificant have taken on a startling new importance. For instance, an entry marked *Hollywood, June 2, 1932,* simply records *Eight-thirty – Preview.* But on that night Jean Harlow and Charles Boyer, two unknown movie actors, zoomed into stardom and my own life was turned over like an upside-down cake.

I grant that the short entries in a datebook can sometimes pose a mystery. In Santa Monica, July 4, 1935, I scribbled : *Leave for New York. Lend beach house to Joe.* And then, six weeks later, a mystery comes to light : *Home from vacation. Find house in order except for FOOTPRINTS ON THE CEILING.*

Only Hollywood could supply an answer to that mystery. Joe Schenck was an eminent film producer, and, in spite of girth, advancing years, and retreating hairline, he dearly loved to play. And I learned on investigation that those footprints had come about during a beach party Joe gave. It seemed that Johnny Weissmuller, the current 'Tarzan,' had grabbed a starlet, whose feet were smeared with suntan oil, and hoisted her, upside down, until she was walking on the ceiling.

I also find those old datebooks useful in exposing some event I once considered earth-shaking. One night I kept a rendezvous with a sophisticated European film director which I, as a Hollywood novice, found so unforgettable it only needed be recorded with a fingerprint in lipstick. Had I written that occasion up 'in depth' when it took place, it would have been a pack of lies because today I can't remember his name to give him a belated screen credit. So I'm against diaries and all for datebooks, because memory is more indelible than ink.

One day in 1927 I scribbled down an ordinary run-of-the-mill tea date but I met a character that afternoon who was to dominate my life as long as he lived. His name was Wilson Mizner. In 1936 he became the inspiration for a movie I wrote starring Clark Gable, Jeanette MacDonald, and the San Francisco earthquake. Its title was *San Francisco* and it still runs on the late TV shows.

In 1926 I'd given up my writing career to live a private life with the husband I then adored. John Emerson was twenty years my senior; handsome, literate, and educated for the clergy. When he deserted the church to invade Broadway, he perfected that charisma, which even a bad actor has, of being able to charm his off-stage public.

In time John Emerson rose to be a featured player for Broadway's distinguished theatrical producer, Charles Frohman. In 1909, when the playwright Clyde Fitch died leaving his tragedy *The City* unfinished, John completed the manuscript and brought the play through to a successful run. John played leading roles with Minnie Maddern Fiske, America's most serious theatrical star; he co-authored and starred in a successful whodunit called *The Conspiracy*. Then, sensing the new opportunities that were opening up on the

West Coast, he cast a glance toward Hollywood with a view to directing films.

D. W. Griffith had always looked down on movies as a bastard child of the theater, and when a distinguished figure like John Emerson approached him for a job, he was flattered. He immediately asked John to join his staff of directors.

Another of D. W.'s importations was a handsome Broadway juvenile named Douglas Fairbanks. While John was learning to direct by watching D. W. at work, Doug was being cast in several rather pedestrian roles in which he failed to register. And Doug, homesick for Broadway, began marking time to get back there.

It didn't take John Emerson long to master the new technique and then, feeling that Griffith had overlooked Fairbanks's potential, he decided that his first film would exploit the young actor's dashing personality.

John Emerson started a search through the files in the scenario department to find a vehicle for Fairbanks. The studio purchased a good many action-stories which had appeared in pulp magazines, but one day Emerson unearthed a file of plots that I had concocted directly for the screen.

Over a hundred of my half-hour slapstick comedies had already been filmed. I still have two of those old manuscripts; the first dating back to 1914 was titled *The Deadly Glass of Beer*. It starred the character actor Tully Marshall and was directed by Tod Browning, who later rose to be master of the macabre in early film art. (His movie *Freaks* opened up a new genre of horror films long before Hitchcock.)

The Deadly Glass of Beer earned me $25, not bad in those days for a synopsis written on a single page.

THE DEADLY GLASS OF BEER

Henry and Frank are cousins who meet at a lawyer's office to hear their uncle's will read. The will states: 'I leave one million dollars to my nephew Frank if by his twenty-first birthday he has remained a strict teetotaler. But if Frank should drink even a single glass of beer, my entire fortune is to go to Henry.' Henry, smothering his fury, plots Frank's downfall.

Disguised by false whiskers, Henry trails Frank about town in the hope of catching him taking a drink. One day Frank passes a saloon, hesitates, furtively looks up and down the street, and ducks in. Henry follows him into the saloon, grabs off his false whiskers, raps Frank on the back, and says, 'Aha! I've caught you!' At which Frank turns around and shows his glass to be full of buttermilk.

The day before Frank's twenty-first birthday, Henry becomes desperate. Aided by cohorts, he kidnaps Frank and takes him to a den on the waterfront. There he is strapped to a table; his mouth is propped open and Henry is about to pour a bottle of beer into Frank when, just as the clock strikes twelve, the police break in and arrest Henry for serving liquor without a license.

Are you ready for another example of those primitive beginnings out of which grew the first new Art Form since Time began?

A GIRL LIKE MOTHER

Maude is in love with Sidney, a youth who has sworn he will never wed until he finds 'a girl like Mother.' In an attempt to learn what sort of girl his mother is, Maude frequents Sidney's neighborhood to study her from a distance. But through an unfortunate error, she mistakes the town trollop for Sidney's mother. Although it goes against the grain of a modest girl like

Maude, she proceeds to whoop it up in a manner that ruins forever any chance to win the man she loves.

In the denouement, however, Maude explains that her rowdy behavior was due to her great love for Sidney and that she is, indeed, 'a girl like Mother.'

Studying those synopses in the script department that day, John Emerson began to think that their humor had a refreshing impudence. Presently he came across a story that poked fun at our American aristocracy. It had been inspired by Hollywood's neighboring community of Pasadena, a winter resort for snobbish families whose lineage had been established by brand names such as Heinz's Pickles, Smith Brothers' Cough Drops, and Chalmers' Underwear. My hero, in disgrace because he added nothing to the family *réclame*, is threatened with disinheritance unless, by hook or crook, he begins to get *His Picture in the Papers* (which was the title of my story).

Looking for the author's name, John Emerson found it to be 'A. Loos.' For, when I first began to submit manuscripts, I had a theory they'd get more consideration if their author seemed to be a man.

John Emerson hurried to report to Griffith: 'There's some fellow named Loos who's turned out just what I want for a Fairbanks picture. When can I meet him?' With a glint in his eye, D. W. said, 'Right now,' and ordered A. Loos to be fetched from the script department.

But he then proceeded to warn Emerson that the script he had picked out was deceptive. 'If you study it,' Griffith said, 'you'll notice that most of the laughs are in the dialogue which can't be photographed.' When Emerson asked why he bought the stories, D. W. said because they made *him* laugh. Emerson ventured they might do the same for audiences if the laugh-lines were printed on the film. 'But people don't go to the movies to read,' Griffith argued.

When I appeared in answer to D. W.'s summons, John Emerson was astonished that A. Loos was a small brunette in a sailor suit with hair hanging down her back in a long braid. On my part, I was not impressed by my discoverer. Unaware that he was one of Broadway's most distinguished citizens, I thought he looked rather a fogy.

I accepted an invitation to go to the corner drugstore for a soda and there went through an intensive questioning about the slapstick comedies I was turning out for the second-string directors at the studio. 'Wouldn't you like someone to film one of those satires you've written?' asked Mr Emerson. 'Maybe,' I told the old boy, 'but Mr Griffith says they won't work.'

It wasn't easy to get D. W.'s okay to film my story, but he finally agreed and at the same time warned Emerson to finish the picture before Doug's option came due, because the studio was going to let him go. Following Emerson's instructions, I wrote my plot in full detail, and included a lot of subtitles.

We filmed our picture with a great deal of spontaneous horseplay on the part of Doug, some of which John included in the movie. During this time D. W., deeply involved in his major work *Intolerance*, allowed us to float our trial balloon without paying it any attention.

Not until our movie was cut and titled were we able to snare Griffith into a projection room to see what we'd done. D. W. viewed those subtitles with grudging attention, and, at the end, he made one shattering comment. 'Your idea doesn't work, Mr Emerson. We'll have to shelve the picture.'

We filed out of the projection room in dark despair, not knowing that, by a lucky error in the shipping department, a copy of *His Picture in the Papers* had already been shipped to the New York Exchange.

In the New York of those days, the Roxy Movie Palace was managed by S. L. Rothapfel, a show-biz character who could have been an invention of Dickens. He was fat, rosy, and bald, and considered himself the host of each and every soul who bought a ticket. Every Monday morning found him in the foyer, receiving guests for the premiere of his new show. 'Hi, Roxy! How's the movie this week?' some fan might ask. Roxy told the truth even when painful. 'Well, Mack, the film may be a little gushy, but Blanche Sweet's a doll!'

Well, Fate had decreed that on a certain Monday morning Roxy's new feature hadn't yet been delivered by the Exchange. In a panic, he phoned to demand, 'Where the hell's my show? It's almost opening time!' It was apparent that something must have happened to the delivery truck but Roxy was assured the Exchange would immediately rush over a substitute. 'Yeah?' he asked in derision. 'Who's the star?' 'A new young actor named Doug Fairbanks.' 'Fine thing,' barked Roxy. 'I advertise Eddy Dillon, and then insult my customers with a nobody.'

Roxy faced that opening day audience to announce, with hollow geniality, that there'd been a temporary switch in the program. 'But hold your horses. I'll put the feature on just as soon as it gets here.' Then Roxy beat a retreat and hoped for the best.

His *Picture in the Papers* started to unroll, beginning with a long subtitle, which was a highly unusual procedure. Movie titles up to that time had been strictly informative and very brief: 'The Next Day,' 'That Same Evening,' or at their most literate, 'Came the Dawn.' Roxy was both surprised and relieved when the opening title brought forth a hearty laugh.

Then, as one subtitle after another flashed on the screen, the laughter mounted until the audience was roaring with gusty approval. And Roxy, standing at the back of the house, realized he was present at a startling innovation.

It is difficult to imagine the impact those written words had on that early-day audience. And next morning the movie critic of *The New York Times* said, in essence, 'satire has invaded the screen; the movies are growing out of their infancy.'

When, halfway through the picture, one of Roxy's minions reached his side to say the missing film had arrived, Roxy trotted down the aisle, climbed to the stage, and raised his hand to stop the picture. 'Listen, children, the regular film just got here. Do you want me to yank Doug Fairbanks?' 'No! No! No!' came a reply that sounded like thunder. The picture continued to a hilarious end, by which time Doug Fairbanks had put an entire audience permanently into his pocket.

That movie lifted Doug into instant stardom; D. W. took up his option, assigned John Emerson as Doug's permanent director, and put me on as sole writer for the Fairbanks unit. (Note to Women's Lib : I need never have signed my name 'A. Loos.') Moreover, D. W. was quick to admit his mistake about the written word on film. He ordered me to write a full set of subtitles for *Intolerance*. One that I filched from Voltaire stated that when women cease to attract men, they take to noble deeds to gain attention. It still gets a laugh.

Working with John Emerson turned out to be great fun and I began to realize he was anything but a fogy. In fact, Doug never ceased kidding about his affairs with glamorous Broadway stars, among whom were Fay Bainter and the delectable Billie Burke.

Jealousy entered the scene when Emily Stevens arrived in Los Angeles on a starring tour in *Hedda Gabler*. A full-blown, red-headed beauty, she made me feel pretty insignificant.

Moreover, she was so possessive of John that he even neglected our work ... a little. How could I ever have considered him a fogy?

But even stronger than jealousy was the fact that John enjoyed frail health, which brings out the mother in a girl and is an extremely sexy emotion. As for John, he must have felt rejuvenated, after years of knocking about Broadway, to have a little Hollywood sweetheart who not only catered to his every demand, but also brought home a great deal of bacon.

At one point during our collaboration, John took leave of absence from Doug to make a picture without me. It was a story of India starring Mary Pickford, and it turned out to be the first failure America's Sweetheart ever made. Although the disaster was blamed on a bad script, it was shattering to John's ego and also evidence of how necessary I'd become to his career. At any rate, he asked me to marry him. That an unsophisticated girl like me could take a man-of-the-world away from Emily Stevens was intoxicating. And I became Mrs John Emerson, confident that that delirious state would last forever.

Working with Doug continued to seem like child's play and, at the same time, it was making us rich. John always took charge of my earnings and, investing our salaries in the foolproof stock market of the Twenties, he began to stack up a fortune. But, in the opinion of Broadway, movies still belonged to the category of comic strips, which destroyed John's pride in his film career. And, looking about for a praiseworthy side line, he began to involve himself in left-wing politics, as wealthy show-biz types often do.

At the same time, we both recognized that Southern California had become a dumping ground for kooks, weirdos, and incompetents who set its pace and created its cultural atmosphere. So, after accumulating money enough, we quit

Hollywood forever (or so we thought) and took up residence in New York.

John was immediately welcomed as an eloquent speech-maker for the Actors' Equity Association in its battle with theater managers for better working conditions. In the ensuing Actors' Equity strike, John quickly rose to be a leader. The striking actors, because of their glamour, made headlines all over the country. It was an exhilarating new life for an ex-movie director who had been ashamed of his job. But it was a life in which I, alas, was no longer needed.

Trying to fight off chagrin over my husband's neglect, I gradually drifted into a set of intellectuals whose IQ was as high as their talk was rowdy: H. L. Mencken, Ernest Boyd, the Irish essayist, Joseph Hergesheimer, and George Jean Nathan. I also made new girl friends : Tallulah Bankhead and Adele Astaire, who were incomparable fun, and Zoe Akins, the playwright and poetess who lived for romance and for food, never recognizing that too much heft nullified her prospects for l'amour.

But much as I appreciated those friends, I could also laugh at them. And prompted by a flirtation that Henry Mencken was having with a stupid little blonde, I wrote a skit poking fun at his romance. I had no thought of it ever being printed; my only purpose was to make Henry laugh at himself, which it did.

In 1925 my spoof found its way into print under the title of *Gentlemen Prefer Blondes*. It was published first as a serial in *Harper's Bazaar*; after which it ran into 85 editions as a book, followed by 14 translations, including one in Chinese which was serialized in a newspaper published by Lin Yutang. (When I met Dr Lin and asked how the book could be understood by a race that has no blondes, he said, 'My dear young lady, blondness is not restricted to pigmentation. And your dialogue fits quite naturally into the argot of our Sing-Song girls.')

From the beginning, my tough little blonde proved to be a healthy financial enterprise. But I never had to bother my head with business, for John, as usual, took my money as soon as it came in.

And if Women's Lib wants to make an issue of that situation, let me speak up for all the girls like me who automatically hand their wages over to a man. Our type was later to be described in a lyric that Leo Robin wrote for the brunette in the musical version of my book.

I LOVE WHAT I'M DOING

I love what I'm doing when I'm doing it for love
The kick that I get is my reward
If a boy is not a spender
I'm inclined to be more tender
And believe you me I'm never bored.

I love what I'm doing when I'm doing it for love
I know every bench in Central Park
If a lad who comes a-wooing
Wants to take me out canoe-ing
It's the greatest thing since Noah's Ark.
And if a guy takes me out riding
And his motor car breaks down
I roll up my sleeves and help him shove
But I'm really in my hey-day
If he wants ten bucks till pay day
'Cause I love what I'm doing when I'm doing it for love.

It isn't for nothing that one of America's most poignant love songs, 'My Man,' glorifies a character who isn't very faithful to his girl.

The day finally came when I discovered a letter from one of John's fellow socialists, expressing her joy over being able to compensate for his unfulfilled marriage. When faced with that evidence, John disarmed me by bursting into tears. He bitterly regretted that he wasn't the marrying type; that he had never wanted children; that his nerves were shattered by such a binding arrangement.

Tremulous with guilt over having made a great big grown man weep, I asked if he wanted a divorce. He grasped me in agitation. 'No, no, no, Buggie! I'll never leave you; you're so gullible you might fall into the hands of some crook who'd get hold of your money!' As an upshot John worked out a friendly separation and granted me an allowance. 'This arrangement will be much better for you, Buggie,' he explained. 'Because in the past you've always had to ask me for money. But now I'm giving my Bug some of her very own.'

John found me an apartment on East Seventy-ninth Street and then moved into bachelor quarters some twenty blocks away. More or less resigned, I settled for a sort of father-daughter relationship during which I affectionately gave John the nickname by which everybody called him from that time on – Mister E.

I was chagrined over my failure as a wife but Mr E.'s plan had one advantage. I at once purchased the mink coat I could have bought years before, but Mr E. never felt he could afford. And thus our carefree way of life continued until 1929 when, all of a sudden, the stock-market crash brought instant privation to millions, foremost among them Mr E.

But after the first few days of panic, Mr E., as usual, became a realist. 'There's enough left from our disaster to support one of us,' he told me. 'Naturally, I'll have to count every penny. But my Bug's in luck because she's healthy and can go to work.'

Now that I was to start writing again, I suddenly realized how much I'd missed it; that, to me, writing had been an absorbing game – something like jigsaw puzzles. It was fun to assemble a group of characters based on people I knew, and then set them against one another for better or worse. And what satisfaction when my game worked out!

Elated at going back to work again, I was all for laying in a stack of yellow pads and a box of pencils, but Mr E. was alarmed. 'No, no, Buggie! Let's face it, writing's a risky business and you might never be lucky again. You'll have to find some job that pays an immediate salary.' It appeared that he'd been mulling over his problem and, as usual, come up with a solution. 'This is your opportunity for a career in something you've always loved ... a career in fashion. A cute little girl like my Bug can easily land a modeling job.'

It was true that, next to writing, I loved clothes. I'd recently posed for *Vogue* and *Harper's Bazaar* in my dresses from Mainbocher. As always, I felt that Mr E. was right. But, on investigation, he found that, like all luxury trades, fashion was dead. There was nothing to do but dip into the capital on which Mr E. had counted for his own future. And then, with poverty drawing closer and closer, there suddenly came out of left field an offer from MGM for me to write a movie script at $3500 a week!

Mr E. was staggered, for in New York the entertainment industry was moribund. New Yorkers have an adage: 'As Wall Street goes, so does Broadway.' And Broadway was dying. (It's always dying. In 1974 it's dying again.) But strangely enough, motion-picture houses throughout the nation were jammed. Folks were skimping on the bare necessities of life to buy distraction. Not only did films survive the crash but Hollywood was just entering its zenith.

While Mr E. felt his Buggie might not make good in the talkies, my salary was guaranteed for six months. I, myself, wasn't able to figure that sum out but it was large enough for Mr E. to let me take up my pencil again.

December 11, 1931, found me at Grand Central Station in New York, waiting to board the crack Twentieth Century Limited. At long last I was going back to California : where I was born, where my career began in those early silent films, and where the Loos family was still entrenched. Mr E. came to the station to see me off and, as the conductor called 'All aboard,' he detained me long enough for final instructions : 'Don't fall for Clark Gable when you get out there, Buggie dear. Remember your old boy lives only for his little Bug !'

That declaration might have seemed a bit crass under the circumstances, for I had long realized that Mr E.'s devotion was largely affected by the amount of money I earned. But the transparent means he took to conceal that fact had grown into a joke which I could only enjoy. And, as every Don Juan knows, we girls are so eager for compliments a man needn't try to be subtle. At any rate, it was his sweet talk I'd fallen for in the beginning.

2

Once Again the Caveman

MR E. was actually the forerunner of a type that was beginning to emerge in our country. From early Colonial days, sex life in America had been based on the custom of men supporting women. That situation reached its heyday in the Twenties when it was easy for any dabbler in stocks to flaunt his manhood by lavishing an unearned income on girls. But with the stock-market crash, men were hard put even to keep their wives, let alone spend money on sex outside their home. The adjustment was much easier on women than on men, who jumped out of windows in droves, whereas I can't recall a single headline that read: KEPT GIRL LEAPS FROM LOVE NEST.

All over the nation girls started to earn their own money. Gold diggers whose lives had been the most tedious, readily took to exciting jobs as mannequins, models, and cover girls. Those with sufficient talent went on the stage. Nontalented beauties got jobs in Hollywood and the nonbeauties went into offices.

Soon a type of husband emerged who, like Mr E., required his wife to contribute to their support. And a new social order went into effect throughout the entire country. Men began to put a greater value on their services to women.

In New York, parents of debutantes had to entice young men into stag lines by offering free transportation to and from the Colony Club; they had to provide free theater tickets, night-club entertainment, and other diversions. In humbler circles the Dutch treat was established; escorts required a girl to pay for half their date and they didn't even flinch when she offered to foot the entire bill, although in the beginning she was frequently told to pass the money under the table. Presently, men took to dipping into a girl's wages and the kept man began to emerge in America.

In our country males of that type had generally been stigmatized by a term that would have caused the gold digger of the Twenties to shudder ... to her predatory way of thinking it was the most shocking of all four-letter words ... pimp.

But as a connoisseur of that species I would like to come to its defense. In European culture it is quite respectable for women to support men. In the case of marriage, it is done by the *dôt* (or dowry) system where a husband is subsidized before the ceremony. No European male is ever humiliated by having to go to his wife holding out his hat. Only in the crude culture of the New World was the kept man considered decadent.

Actually the system is a very healthy return to the primal relationship between the sexes, when a man went out to hunt and his mate trudged behind lugging the stone hatchet needed for the kill. That custom had definite rewards; for after a woman had dragged home the prey, skinned it, cooked supper, and tidied the cave, she had proved herself worthy of her man's affection and its consummation became a triumphant payoff. Pleasure that isn't paid for is as insipid as everything else that's free.

Throughout the tenderloins of the world, where life is geared to the understanding of sex, a code has been established that the girls must have one man to whom they give their all, or they'll never take any satisfaction in their work. To paraphrase Lorelei Lee, 'A kiss on the hand makes a girl feel respected, but a smack in the face denotes ardor.'

It is quite likely that American women have long had an atavistic hunger for that sort of mistreatment without ever realizing it. In late years push-button housekeeping has so reduced their work that they find no way to exercise their emotions. But women should now take heart that our country has entered full-swing into a more vital way of life; one which provides the American woman with a sex experience she never had before; the thrill of 'giving' instead of 'taking.'

A wide variety of kept or semikept men has developed since the disappearance of the gold digger of the Twenties. In cases where a girl has talent, any husband or lover can 'manage' her career, and, although he generally mucks it up thoroughly, he's able to save face, which makes him an amiable mate.

Then there is the type who takes credit for his mate's achievements. A classic example was that of the great French writer, Colette, whose husband, Willy, put his name on her work as co-author.

In any service where a couple hold down jobs as a team, the male generally takes his ease while the wife labors at his job as well as her own.

There is the hypochondriac who alibis his pimpery by trumped-up ailments.

There is the aristocrat whose social position is an adequate exchange for room, board, and pocket money.

Then there is a bargain type of pimpery where the most forlorn and sex-starved little woman can enjoy the society of Marlon Brando or Richard Burton by paying only a pittance of their colossal salaries at a box office.

But pimping is not always practiced for money; there is another and much more unattainable commodity. A famous case in Hollywood was that of William Randolph Hearst, who squandered more on making a star of artless little Marion Davies than was spent on both Pompadour and Du Barry.

But Hearst remained none-the-less a predator, for, in return, he was getting something that money seldom buys. Hearst was given back his youth through Marion's childish antics, energy, and zest for laughter. Their relationship was much the same as that between sparkling Wallis Windsor and the mate who was so lacking in vitality. And so the two greatest love stories of our time were provided by women who 'gave' without stint and men who 'took.'

But first and foremost among pimps is the basic type who glories in his disregard for women. Jimmy Cagney, in a film, provided catharsis to a world of pampered females by shoving half a grapefruit into his Baby's face; Humphrey Bogart, with exquisite procrastination, issued the famous order, 'Play it, Sam!' which in my mind kept a torrid sweetheart waiting.

That same type has been glorified in a great play by Henrik Ibsen. Its hero, Peer Gynt, after being unfaithful to his wife in several countries of Europe, returns home at long last, to say grudgingly, 'I'm sorry.'

'But why be sorry, Peer?' asks Solveig. 'Waiting for you has made my whole life a beautiful dream!'

In recent years there have been several real-life charmers who can vie with Peer Gynt. Aly Khan, the Ismailian potentate, seduced hundreds of girls and then broke with them but never lost the adoration of a single victim. Then there was the masterful Adam Clayton Powell, who never apologized for bad behavior, never explained, never regretted, and left female Harlem weeping when he died.

Near the top of my own list is Mike Todd, the hot-shot Broadway producer. He once broke a contract with me but touched my heart by his impudence. 'Look, sweetheart, I'm playing it as straight with you as any Broadway hustler can!' And when Gypsy Rose Lee starred in Mike's hit revue, Star and Garter, he 'borrowed' her life's savings and then ran out on her. But the day Mike was killed in a plane crash en route to join his bride, Liz Taylor, Gypsy called me up, sobbing her very heart out. 'Oh, Nita, there'll never be another man like Mike!'

James Barrie has written that charm is the bloom on a woman; if she has it she doesn't need anything more. In the same manner bravado can be the bloom on a man. He doesn't need anything more.

Well – back in the Gay Nineties Wilson Mizner was at the beginning of a career of superb bravado. Six-foot four and handsome as Adonis, he swaggered into New York's Claridge Hotel one midnight, in top hat and Inverness, accompanied by Bessie McCoy, the toast of Broadway. Both were unaware that the middle-aged socialite who sponsored Wilson stood on the balcony above them waiting to brand him with the four-letter name she couldn't force her aristocratic lips to utter.

As an alternative she called out, 'Listen everybody! I want all New York to know Wilson Mizner for what he really is!' Then, using the same method by which Armand Duval let Paris know that Marguerite Gautier took money for her favors, Myra Yerkes unleashed $100,000 in greenbacks down on Wilson's head.

Many years after that avalanche, Wilson told me about it. 'But entertaining a lady for pay is strictly kid-stuff,' Wilson mused. 'There were a lot of other rackets more suitable to a man of talent.'

Well, that day I left for Hollywood, poor Mr E. was doing his best as the type who has to make good by obvious lies. He was putting up a gallant fight, but he knew that his Buggie, a pushover for rogues of every kind, had been swept into the orbit of a man who must go down in the annals of larceny as the most impudent scamp of an entire era. Once aboard the Twentieth Century, I'd be on my way to meet him. Our rendezvous had been made by long-distance phone and was already written in my datebook: *Hollywood December 16. Lunch at the Brown Derby with Wilson Mizner.*

3

The Homefolk of Hollywood

IN 1931 it took five days on two crack trains to get to Hollywood: the Twentieth Century Limited to Chicago and the Santa Fe Super Chief to Los Angeles. But what a de luxe five days! Compartments glittered with polished mahogany, shiny brass, and red brocade; the seats flaunted antimacassars of heavy lace. Gazing out on drab railroad tracks or the flat plains of Kansas doubled one's pleasure in the impeccable service and gourmet food. The maître d'hôtel would come to the compartment to announce he'd acquired some trout caught that morning in an icy mountain stream of Colorado or that the guinea hen had hung for just the proper time.

There was always a steady stream of celebrities; a screen star with her entourage of husband, lover, manager, agent, hairdresser, or maid. Gloria Swanson, as the Countess de la Falaise, might be returning from a holiday in Paris, where a Venetian gondola had been installed as a bed in her suite at the Crillon.

It was a status symbol for girls to receive flirtatious telegrams from husbands or sweethearts along the route. (I knew a waning star who used to send herself telegrams in order to impress the Pullman porter.)

My train had just passed the One hundred and twenty-fifth Street Station when there was a tap on the door of my compartment and it was opened by a distinguished gentleman who said, 'I beg your pardon, but aren't you Spanish?'

His question was apropos of nothing at all; he merely used it for openers to pick up a wind-blown brunette who didn't appear to have the brains of a moth. I recognized his type only too well, having written it up in my book; he was the classic Sugar Daddy, rich, a pushover for expensive presents, and extremely dull company. But he eased his way into my compartment and I finally agreed to dine with him that evening. Oh well . . . a girl can't spend *all* her time with brigands.

Next morning, entering the diner for breakfast, I heard a female voice calling, '*Cou-cou!*' (the French equivalent of 'Yoo hoo!'). I looked over and saw a young woman who appeared vaguely familiar. 'Remember me?' she asked, 'We met at Maxim's in Paris. You were lunching with Georges Carpentier.'

She was Mme Maurice Chevalier and I joined her, happy to be rescued from a possible breakfast with my pickup of the previous evening.

Like the wives of most adorable men, Yvonne Chevalier was nondescript; a small brunette, rather personable without being pretty. Maurice explained in his autobiography that she looked after him tenderly while he was being cured of a youthful drug addiction. Doubtless many prettier girls would have done the job, because Maurice was already the idol of Paris, but Yvonne got there first. And after Maurice was cured, he married her as a reward.

It thrilled Yvonne to boast that she was on the way to join her husband but I figured he needed her in Hollywood just about as much as I'd need Mr E. there. For Maurice was rumored to be in love with his American costar. Their affair had frustrated eavesdroppers, because the lady was born in France, spoke the language as well as Maurice, and the two could talk freely in front of everyone. I don't intend to reveal her name because even at this late date Claudette might resent my letting that cat out of the bag.

The Twentieth Century reached Chicago, where we changed over to the Santa Fe Super Chief for the remainder of the trip. And there Yvonne ran into an acquaintance; a young French actor nobody had ever heard of. Not being clairvoyant I didn't even bother to put his name in my datebook.

In Kansas City, the conductor brought me a telegram from Mr E., reminding me that he was still living only for his Bug. Had he only wired 'I'm still living *on* my Bug,' I'd have adored his impudence and possibly fallen in love with him once more.

On reaching Albuquerque, Yvonne got a telegram from Maurice that she couldn't wait to show me. It contained fond expressions of Parisian hanky-panky; *je t'aime, mille tendresses, je t'attend joyeusement*, etc. But aware of Maurice's integrity, I realized he must have suffered pangs of guilt when he wrote those fibs in order to make Yvonne feel welcome.

On December 14 my datebook states: *Leave train at Pasadena*. The Hollywood cognoscenti always disembarked there in order to avoid the wear and tear of the Los Angeles Station. (Yvonne's young actor friend, being a novice, went on to L.A. and for six months I lost sight of him.)

On disembarking, Yvonne was informed that her famous husband was 'on location' with his costar and 'unable' to meet her, but Maurice had arranged for the Paramount publicity staff to welcome her. After that dubious entry, Yvonne worked hard to fit into the Hollywood scene. She took lessons in English from a lady who taught movie actors to *e-nun-ci-ate* in a manner that Stanislavski would never have tolerated. When Yvonne completed her course, she spoke English in a precise, cultured, and very tiresome manner, from which she would lapse into her own colorful brand of guttersnipe French; a sort of linguistic Dr Jekyll and Mme Hyde.

31

But to whom is correct pronunciation an aphrodisiac? There were plenty of heartaches ahead for Yvonne, who finally gave up, agreed to a divorce, and returned to France. After which the spotlight went off poor little Yvonne forever.

(But now, in 1974, an item clipped in my datebook brings three of my old friends together. 'Paris Jan. 5th [1972]; Maurice Chevalier was buried today ... present at the services was Georges Carpentier, ex-World Heavyweight Champion ... a wreath of red roses bore the words: "Yvonne to Maurice." ')

Zooming back to the Pasadena station, I found my brother Clifford waiting there for me. He remained discreetly in the background while a publicity crew from MGM covered my arrival. I was photographed waving 'Hello' from the car steps and then interviewed, during which time my would-be Sugar Daddy learned he'd been pursuing a female writer. It must have set him back on his heels; for he bade me a very chastened good-by and probably swore off brunettes forever. Then Clifford drove me away in his Cadillac.

Clifford was the family treasure. He was a leader in all civic affairs of southern California and known nationally as one of the pioneers of group medicine. Today, many years after his death, Clifford's name graces an enormous clinic in the heart of Los Angeles. My brother was always as worthy as I was disrespectful, but we shared a strong family resemblance, except that he was tall and handsome. We adored each other and were proud of our disparate achievements, but, truth to tell, we didn't have much in common. Clifford would painstakingly correct anyone who mispronounced our name. I never cared what people called me. So I became Miss 'Loose,' while my brother was always Dr 'Lohse.'

That night, a family reunion was held at Clifford's Spanish hacienda and seated about the dinner table were Mother,

Pop, Clifford, his daughter Mary (a look-alike of Dolores Del Rio), and me, the adventurer from faraway places. They asked a few questions out of politeness but were much more interested in telling me about *their* affairs. Had I boasted of an invitation I'd recently had from President Masaryk to visit him in Prague, Mother might have interrupted to announce that her cat just had kittens. However, a few snatches of our table-talk might be revealing.

CLIFFORD [*making conversation*] : Do you expect that husband of yours to follow you out here, Neetsie?
ME [*with a grin*] : Not if I send him my paycheck every week.
POP: So he can gamble it away on Wall Street, eh?
ME: Now Pop, you can't blame poor Mr E. for the crash!
POP: Just the same, you should stop giving that deadbeat any more money!
MOTHER: Harry dear! You mustn't talk that way. *They're married!*
ME: Mother's right, Pop! Besides, Mr E. would much rather earn his own money! He just isn't smart enough.
POP: He was smart enough to hook you!
ME: Oh well – he could be worse.
POP: I'd like you to explain *how*?
ME: Well, Pop, for one thing, Mr E. isn't the least bit possessive. He never really gives me any trouble.
POP: Because he never gives! *Period!*
MOTHER [*in response to my giggle*] : Now don't laugh, honey bunch! You only encourage your father.

Mother was right as always. Mr E. was much more to be pitied than laughed at. He felt so pathetically sure that everyone accepted him at his own valuation. His image at the moment was that of a brilliant writer forced to turn down a fabulous offer from MGM because of ill-health. 'I made them settle for Buggie in my place,' he explained, 'but of course they realize I'll be giving her my aid.'

In spite of its pathos, the situation had its funny side and I'm reminded of a vaudeville act in which a pompous comedian used to play the William Tell Overture on a xylophone unaware that, behind him, Gypsy Rose Lee was doing a strip tease. As audiences went wild acclaiming Gypsy, the stupid old xylophonist kept taking bows.

I began to feel guilty about that table-talk of ours which, had Mr E. overheard it, would have stabbed him to the heart. So I was grateful when Clifford spoke up and changed the subject.

'Well, Neetsie, how soon do you start work?'

It would be the very next morning.

4

The Talkies Heard a Master's Voice

December 15, 1931 — 10:00 a.m. — Report to
Irving Thalberg

THIS conference would start me on my second-time-round
in films. But Hollywood had gone through drastic changes
since my career began there, writing movie scripts for D. W.
Griffith.

In those thoughtless days none of us ever associated movies
with art; such 'easy money' placed them in the category
of striking oil. D. W. himself was only marking time until
he could go back to being a playwright and a poet.
His previous efforts along those lines had been dismal and
he would never have dreamed he was creating 'art' on film.

When I left D. W. it had been to write the films in which
Douglas Fairbanks soared on his giddy way to fame and
fortune. Doug was now established as a lodestar in the Hollywood firmament but, alas, some of my other associates of the
old days had been felled by the advent of sound. Among them
was Norma Talmadge, who was a vision of romance as long
as she kept her mouth shut. She would have made an ideal
Portia until she announced in her Brooklynese, 'The quality
of moicy . . .'

Another victim of the revolution was John Gilbert. As
great a lover off-screen as he was on, Jack had torrid romances
with a number of film sirens including Greta Garbo. He
had married Ina Claire, the stage star and pet of international society. But like many people of Irish extraction,

Jack could never tone his voice down from a high upper register.

Even in those early days, however, the sound technicians could perform miracles, and had MGM ordered a manly voice for Jack, it might have been achieved. But for some time the studio had felt he was getting too much salary. It's possible his broken romance with Garbo and the fact that Ina Claire divorced him in record time had tarnished his charisma. At any rate, Jack's star was on the wane and his contract still had several years to go. So the technicians were ordered to let Jack speak in tones that indicated he had no love interest in womankind at all.

As soon as Jack Gilbert started to talk on film, his erstwhile fans began to giggle. Nasty little boys called out 'Whoops-a-Daisy,' and 'Look out Jack, your slip's showing!' Not very long after that debacle Jack died. Had anyone asked me what caused his death I'd have answered, 'Hollywood.'

But many of my other friends from the old silent days had made good vocally. Mary Pickford, Lionel Barrymore, Lillian and Dorothy Gish (all four of whom had been in my first filmplay *The New York Hat*) were now flourishing. While it was true that Mary Pickford's Kate in *The Taming of the Shrew* had a faulty cadence, her speech was quite adequate for any typical Mary Pickford role. Doug Fairbanks, too, was a strong link with my past, as were Erich von Stroheim, Charlie Chaplin, Gloria Swanson, and any number of others.

'Hollywood' had now come to be a generic name; most of the studios had moved away from there. I had never seen MGM, which I now found sprawling over a wide expanse in Culver City, the shabby suburb built on a salt marsh leading down to the Pacific. As I got there that morning the sea air was most agreeable but the bright sun only served to show up a hodgepodge of nondescript buildings, some of them merely glorified sheds. They were all painted the same wishy-washy shade of gray. I was directed to an unimpressive main building and there, having entered into my movie career with the great D. W. Griffith himself, I was once more to begin at the top. For Irving Thalberg, a legend even in his short lifetime, stood head and shoulders above every other producer in Hollywood.

While I was seated in his waiting room, an eager little Mickey Mouse of a man wearing pince-nez spectacles entered, nodded at me, did a double-take and disappeared. Soon after a secretary summoned me into the young man's office. He introduced himself as Thalberg's assistant and said his name was Albert Lewin.

Grinning widely, Lewin said he had first taken me for an actress and a contender for the leading role of the film I'd been brought out to write. I now learned it was to be based on a best-selling novel, *Red-Headed Woman* by Katharine Brush, the wicked-lady-novelist of the early 1930s. Lewin informed me that every star, contract player, and extra girl in Hollywood was clamoring to play the title role of that movie. And, although I was a brunette, he had said to himself, With a flashy red wig, why not?

'I'm glad you're a writer,' Lewin told me. 'I'll have a chance to see you more often.' With which typical Hollywood come-on, he escorted me into the presence of the Great Little Master.

This was not my first meeting with Thalberg. I had been indirectly involved with him years ago when, at twenty-one, Irving was the boy genius of Hollywood and head of Universal Studios. At that time I happened to be the scenarist and giggling companion of Constance Talmadge, that sparkling blond clown who, for no reason, went by the nickname of Dutch. Irving, just like film fans all over the country, was wildly in love with her. His courtship, however, was beset by difficulties, for Irving's job was enormously confining and Dutch was a playgirl, negligent of her own career, and unimpressed by a boyish suitor who took work seriously.

Often Irving would leave his studio at a late hour to park his car in front of the Talmadge home in Beverly Hills, where he'd wait in the dark until Dutch got back from some party. Only after her bedroom light went out would Irving give up his vigil over the one girl in Hollywood he could never impress.

I found that Irving's appearance had changed very little since he was Dutch's boyish suitor. In spite of his mounting prestige, Irving was still a rather pathetic figure. He had suffered from a heart ailment since childhood and his natural pallor was intensified by long hours in offices and projection rooms, shut away from the California sunshine. I was enormously touched that the shoulders of Irving's jacket were too obviously padded, in order to make him seem more grown-up and robust.

When we met that morning I'm sure we were both thinking about Dutch, who by then was married to Townsend Netcher, a millionaire playboy whose fortune came from a department store in Chicago. Previously Dutch had married and divorced Allaster MacIntosh, a member of the British aristocracy and playboy companion of the Prince of Wales.

After Dutch left Hollywood, Irving became involved with one of his contract actresses, Norma Shearer.

He was now married to Norma, who couldn't have been more unlike Dutch; haunted by ambition, Norma cared a great deal for Irving's power to create stardom. He had been Pygmalion for some of the world's most fabulous Galateas; such idols as Carole Lombard, Myrna Loy, Jean Harlow, Joan Crawford, Greta Garbo and Dolores Del Rio. But Norma's beauty had several effects among which were eyes that were small and rather close together.

There was a period when Mrs Patrick Campbell, the naughty British actress, was under contract to MGM, not as an actress but to expertise on a certain film that concerned the London of Stella Campbell's heyday. She once encountered Irving on the lot and stopped him to exclaim, 'Oh, Mr Thalberg, I've just met that extraordinary wife of yours with the teensy-weensy little eyes!'

At any rate, Norma was bent on marrying her boss and Irving, preoccupied with his work, was relieved to let her make up his mind. Possibly he looked on her career as a challenge and it is to Irving's credit that, by expert show-manship and a judicious choice of camera angles, he made a beauty and a star out of Mrs Thalberg.

Nepotism was then rampant in Hollywood, but it didn't actually affect the finished product. Films might be slowed up by having to go through the hands of various sons, daughters, nephews, nieces, cousins, and in-laws, but by the time a movie went before the cameras, experts had always been called in to straighten out the snarls. (There was one rather bothersome son-in-law at the Warner Brothers studio of whom Wilson Mizner said 'That boy has set back the status of sons-in-law a hundred years'.)

There was a time when Columbia Pictures imported that skilled craftsman, Augustus Thomas, author of such solid Broadway hits as *The Witching Hour* and *Mrs Leffingwell's Boots*. The boss of Columbia, Harry Cohn, handed Augustus a stack of scripts with wobbly plots and asked if he could set them right. After a weekend, Augustus returned with every plot in apple-pie order. At which Cohn stormed into his office screaming, 'Augustus Thomas has straightened out six plots in only three days. Get the s.o.b. on the first train to New York before he wrecks my family life!'

But even in nepotism, Irving made good. His little sister Sylvia became a workman-like scenarist and Irving turned Norma's brother Doug into a competent sound technician.

Norma loved Irving in her own way but not too long after becoming a widow, she entered into a romance with that prince of gamblers, George Raft. It was beset by hectic scenes in public which were not overlooked by the gossip columnists. But Georgie soon returned to his own kind and Norma safely married the handsome ski instructor who has been devoted to her ever since.

At any rate her marriage to Irving was happy enough. Irving had no need of home-life; nor did Norma. She was too much involved in her career to take time out for love or even fun. Had Irving married Dutch, she might have lured him away from work – which would have been disastrous. His marriage to Norma put him safely in a groove of his own choice.

That December morning in 1931 when my first conference with Irving got under way, he explained why he'd sent for me. It seemed that several of his staff authors had written scripts for *Red-Headed Woman*, but they had only emphasized the fact that it was a pretty banal soap opera. The latest filmplay was by Scott Fitzgerald. 'Scott tried to turn the silly book into a tone poem!' Irving said. 'So I want you to make fun of its sex element just as you did in *Gentlemen Prefer Blondes.*'

I wasn't at all sure I could make good in the talkies. 'Don't give it a thought,' said Irving. 'Little Professor Lewin will guide you.' He gave me a copy of the novel, which I was to read at once and report on the next morning.

As I swished through the anteroom on my way out, my Mickey Mouse friend was waiting with an invitation to lunch in the commissary. I had to decline because of my previous date. But when I mentioned Wilson Mizner, Lewin's face broke into a grin of approval. 'I'd resent any other turn-down,' he said, 'but I only envy you. I love the guy!'

Wilson evoked from men the same warm emotions that are generally lavished on idolized sports champions like Babe Ruth and Joe Namath. I treasure a letter from Henry Mencken which states, 'Wilson Mizner is one of my heroes. Christendom would be a sweeter place if there were more like him.'

5

I Learned about Talkies from Thalberg

NEXT morning, back in Irving's office with Albert Lewin, we immediately got down to business. Irving started to pace in front of his imposing executive desk while he boyishly flipped a big silver dollar. 'Let's first of all decide about the love affair in this story,' he said.

Now, *Red-Headed Woman* concerned a cold-blooded schemer who was out to break up the marriage of the man for whom she worked as secretary. But her tactics were so vulgar that when he fell for them, he automatically became a nitwit. How could there possibly be a love story between such a nonhero and nonheroine?

Well, I learned in time that to Irving Thalberg every film had to be a love story. It wasn't at all necessary for the affair to concern people of the opposite sex. Furthermore, age had nothing to do with the matter. One of Irving's most poignant screen romances was *The Champ*, in which the relationship between Jackie Cooper (aged six) and Wallace Beery (a grizzled sixty) held all the rapture of a love affair. And, in *Mutiny on the Bounty*, starring Clark Gable and Charles Laughton, there would be a rivalry so bitter it could only have been based on the strongest mutual fascination. In *The Sin of Madelon Claudet*, the love affair involved an aging prostitute, Helen Hayes, and her reputable, upstanding son, played by Robert Young.

Irving could spot sublimated sex in any human relationship. And he really didn't have to convince me about the deep emotional rapport that can be attained outside a bed. I had once witnessed more ardent emotions between men at an Elks' Rally in Pasadena than they could ever have felt for the type of woman available to an Elk.

Leaving me with the problem of laughing off that redhead's bad behavior, Irving decided I was to work alone after which Arlie would go over each episode with me and if he approved it, we would bring it to Irving for final criticism.

When he first went to work at MGM, Arlie (as everyone called Lewin) was one of the few members of the Hollywood community with any formal education. The son of Russian immigrants, he had become a professor of English in some small Midwestern college. Fascinated by the movies, Lewin had ventured into Hollywood where, as an oddball in that community without culture, Irving hired him at once.

In dealing with actresses or girl writers, Arlie always contrived to mix love with business, but like most Hollywood executives, his passes were largely verbal, a form of *politesse* to which, in Arlie's case, was added genuine friendship. Just the same, a bit of conversational sex makes a pleasant climate for creative effort and working with Arlie was a lot of fun.

Later on I had other proof that Arlie was a charmer. I had given him a letter of introduction to Janet Flanner in Paris, at the time she was just beginning her forty-year stint as a correspondent for the *New Yorker* magazine. Janet cabled me THANK YOU FOR ARLIE.

It was standard procedure at MGM that Irving might keep an author waiting in his anteroom for years, but he now felt that our movie better be released before that highly forgettable best seller was forgotten. So our conferences took precedence over all other matters.

At a time when most Hollywood movies dealt in contrived situations, Irving insisted that plots grow out of character. Even in the zany farces of the Marx Brothers, Irving insisted on truly human motives such as underlie the shenanigans of Molière and Feydeau and turn horseplay into art. Not that Irving carried out this system consciously. I think it would have astonished him had he lived to see that Groucho and Harpo Marx would be regarded as confreres by such men of genius as Stravinsky and Picasso. Genius really makes the most entertaining bedfellows.

Irving's films never dealt in pornography; his chief requirement was to show two lovers in some sort of a guileless romp with all their clothes on. Even in the script Irving prepared for *Camille*, which was to be graced with the steaming presence of Greta Garbo, the love scenes featured tenderness, not passion. (Irving didn't live to supervise the filming of that picture, but Bernie Hyman, his adoring disciple, meticulously followed the spirit of Irving's scenario.)

Irving's insistence that we find a love affair in our story posed some pretty stiff problems. One day I told him in despair, 'If you ever make a movie of *Frankenstein*, you'll try to prove he had a mad crush on the monster he created!' 'Why not?' he asked. 'That old yarn is about due for a new twist.'

(N.B. Again was Irving right. Over forty years later I find in my datebook: 'Tea with Chris Isherwood and Don Bachardy.' And during tea, Chris happened to remark, 'Don and I are writing a filmplay based on *Frankenstein*. We're giving it a new twist by establishing a human relationship between Frankenstein and his monster.')

Just the same, I still questioned whether there could be a love affair in our movie. Irving went on pacing and tossing his silver dollar. Finally he stopped.

'I think I know what the love story can be. Our heroine must be deeply in love with herself.'

'I'd call that pretty unsympathetic,' ventured Arlie.

'But why? The poor girl has the flashy type of looks that frighten off any man with the qualities of a hero. Who is there for her to love, when she only attracts fools?'

Once Irving reached a conclusion, it seemed as though it should have been apparent from the beginning. And with his judgment to guide me, I completed the script in four months which, at MGM, proved to be a record.

However, long before I'd been put on the script, Irving had ordered the publicity department to play up a search for his redhead. But he told me one day that he'd already made up his mind that the most likely contender was a young actress he'd just seen in the Howard Hughes movie *Hell's Angels*. She played a femme fatale who smoked cigarettes in long holders and drove men wild, just as Theda Bara had done for the previous generation.

Irving was undeterred by some scathing criticisms of the girl's talent. Robert Sherwood, later to become one of America's foremost playwrights, was then movie critic on the old version of *Life* magazine and he wrote Jean up as 'an obstreperously alluring young lady named Jean Harlow of whom not much is likely to be heard.'

The only doubt Irving had about the sinister young actress was whether she could be funny.

On the day of Miss Harlow's first meeting with Irving, he asked me to his office to help make an appraisal of her. Jean's own tawny hair had been bleached to a 'platinum' blonde, but she'd been ordered to the make-up department to be fitted with a red wig. She looked about sixteen and her baby-face seemed utterly incongruous against the flaming wig.

Jean didn't seem at all nervous in the presence of the man who could skyrocket her into fame; she had that sort of gently sardonic attitude that comes from having gone through the many ups-and-downs of any budding career in the studios.

Irving, being self-removed from life, dearly loved gossip. 'How did you make out with Howard Hughes?' he asked Jean.

'Well, one day when he was eating a cookie he offered me a bite.' When we laughed, Jean interrupted. 'Don't underestimate that,' she said. 'The poor guy's so frightened of germs, it could darn near have been a proposal!'

'Do you think you can make an audience laugh?' asked Irving.

'With me or at me?'

'At you!'

'Why not? People have been laughing at me all my life.' As Jean breezed out of the office, she stopped at the door to give us a quick, bright little nod, a gesture I wrote into the script and still look for every time I see that old movie.

'I don't think we need worry about Miss Harlow's sense of humor,' said Irving.

Next came the choosing of a director and let me here report that few of those MGM directors were very good. With Irving in charge, there was no necessity for them to have much talent. To direct *Red-Headed Woman*, Irving picked on a favorite crony, Jack Conway. He handed our script to Jack, told him to read it, and meet with us the following day.

When Jack showed up at the conference next morning, he tossed our script onto Irving's desk and said, 'I'll direct this if you insist, but take my word, Irving, people are going to laugh at it.' When asked in amazement what Jack thought our intention was, he was confused. 'Look folks,' said he, 'if you're *trying* to be funny, I'm here to report that a girl like that almost broke up my home once, and believe me it was no joke!' Irving patiently explained that our heroine was

46

not bent on wrecking the career of any Albert Einstein. 'Her victim is as big a dunce as ...' 'As *me?*' Jack ventured with a squirm. 'You hit the nail right on the head!' said Irving. Jack grinned and accepted the assignment. 'But just to be safe,' said Irving, 'I'll have Nita stay on the set to keep reminding you that the picture's a comedy.'

January 22 – 9:30 – Report to set

Sitting with Jean while a technical crew adjusted the lighting, I began to learn something about her street-urchin personality. 'I love people to think I came up from the gutter,' she remarked. 'Wouldn't it be dull to know that my Grandpa's present to me on my *fifth* birthday was an ermine bedspread?'

Jean had been an only child. Her real name was Harlean Carpentier, and the family lived in Kansas City where any wealthy grandpa might think of a five-year-old in terms of ermine bedspreads. At sixteen, she had married one of the town's rich playboys. They had drifted to Los Angeles where Harlean, incapable of being a housewife, took a new name and started to work as an extra in the movies.

Underlying Jean's raffish sense of humor was a resignation unusual for one so young. Nothing would ever surprise Jean. She knew exactly how people were going to react to her; if men were stupid they'd fall for her; if they had good sense, they'd laugh her off.

Now there is a certain type of sex-pot who is not resented by women; Constance Talmadge and Marilyn Monroe were like that. But women were invariably catty toward Jean; largely through a *noblesse oblige* on her part. Jean agreeably supplied them with the shocks they expected.

I recall an occasion on the set where the camera was to

cease grinding abruptly at a moment when Jean started to remove her jacket. But for some reason the boy in charge of the clap-board failed to give the signal to cut, so Jean 'innocently' continued to take off her jacket, under which she was nude to the waist. Nudity was rarely seen in those days, and Jean's had the startling quality of an alabaster statue. Visitors on the set scarcely believed their eyes. The lighting crew almost fell out of the flies in shock. Wide-eyed in her 'apology,' Jean addressed the director. 'I'm sorry, but nobody gave the order to cut.'

Jean and I were together a lot during the filming of *Red-Headed Woman*. One sequence took place on the merry-go-round at the Santa Monica pier. And, as Jack Conway was busy filming another segment of the script, I went out with Jean and directed the scene – my first and last attempt at directing.

Every MGM movie was taken out to one of the Los Angeles suburbs for a preview, Irving being the first producer to make use of audiences for constructive criticism. At each preview, postcards were distributed with a request for the audience to mail in suggestions. Irving paid small attention to professional critics, putting them down as impersonal theorists; but he read those postcards with the greatest respect, and, guided by them, he would re-edit the movie. In some cases no retakes at all were required but there were times when those amateur critics demanded as much as a third of the film to be reshot; a procedure which Irving never hesitated to follow. In those days MGM released a new picture every week: fifty-two movies a year, and every one a success – all due to the fact that Irving took the trouble to find out what pleased audiences and then gave it to them.

The initial preview of *Red-Headed Woman* took place

in Glendale on that momentous date in June of 1932. Irving and I hid out in that suburban audience with our ears nervously tuned for its reaction. And during the first ten minutes we were deeply disturbed, for the audience was as confused as Jack Conway had been. It didn't know whether to laugh at our sex pirate or not, and, as every producer of comedy knows, a half-laugh is worse than none at all. Only after the movie was well along did the audience catch on and begin to enjoy the jokes.

There was no need to wait for postcards on that movie. Irving called me to his office the first thing next morning. 'Look,' said he, 'I'd like you to contrive a prologue which will tip the audience off that the movie's a comedy.' I proceeded to concoct a scene which showed Jean describing to her girl friend the all-abiding depth of her love for her married boss; as proof of which Jean revealed a photo of her loved one on a flashy dime-store garter.

Our second preview was in Pasadena and the movie started off with the garter scene. That did it! Laughs began at once and never ceased to mount to the end of the film.

When *Red-Headed Woman* was released, it instantly catapulted Jean Harlow into stardom. The picture enjoyed all sorts of fringe successes. It won the award of *Vanity Fair* magazine as the best film of the year; and the London office of MGM reported that the royal family kept a copy at Buckingham Palace for entertaining guests after dinner. Among its many distinctions, *Red-Headed Woman* made film history because it brought on more stringent censorship and caused massive difficulties to the industry for years to come. It outraged ladies' clubs throughout the land, but not because of any episode which might be termed salacious. It was because our heroine, the bad girl of whom all good husbands dream, ended her career as many such scalawags do, rich, happy, and respected, without ever having paid for her sin.

Now, one of the adventures of our heroine was a scene in which she was driven home from a shopping tour by a handsome young chauffeur who, laden with packages, respectfully followed her upstairs to her bedroom. But after dropping the packages onto a chaise longue, the chauffeur took his red-headed employer in his arms and kissed her in a long, slow fade-out.

The role of that chauffeur, although short, was important, and one morning Irving sent for me to discuss the casting of the part. 'We've got a French actor here on a six-month option,' said Irving, 'but I'm letting him go because nobody can understand that guy's English. His option is up in two weeks, which would be just long enough for him to do the part of that chauffeur. So take a look at his test and tell me if you think it's worth a rewrite to make the chauffeur a Frenchman.'

When I looked at the tests in the projection room, I recognized the young actor as the friend of Yvonne Chevalier whom I had met on the Santa Fe. So! Now he was to be sent back home to Paris ... one more heart broken by Hollywood.

But I figured the young man's accent wouldn't be too big a problem since his actions were a lot more understandable than words. So he was put into that bit part, in which he finished out his contract and left for Paris, thinking he'd shaken the stardust of Hollywood from his feet forever.

Sometime later, when Irving and I were going through the postcards from those previews, we found a startling unanimity. Not since the days of Rudolph Valentino had any actor made such an impact on the female audience as had that Frenchman who played the tiny part of Jean's chauffeur. None of us involved in the picture was aware of that young actor's power to enchant. It took those suburban housewives to advise Irving that his French accent was even an asset.

Irving immediately cabled the Paris office to send the actor back to Hollywood. His salary, while under option, had been $350 a week. His new contract called for ten times that figure on a two-year guarantee. And for Charles Boyer that was merely the beginning.

6

Christmas, Christmas Everywhere and Not a Drop of Snow

DECEMBER 1931 was drawing to a close and Hollywood was aglow with Christmas spirit, undaunted by sizzling sunshine, palm trees, and the dry encircling hills that would never feel the kiss of snow. But the 'Know-how' that would transform the Chaplin studio into the frozen Chilkoot Pass could easily achieve a white Christmas.

In Wilson's Rolls-Royce convertible, we drove past Christmas trees heavy with fake snow. An entire estate on Fairfax Avenue had been draped in cotton batting; carolers straight out of Dickens were at its gate, perspiring under mufflers and greatcoats. The street signs on Hollywood Boulevard had been changed to Santa Claus Lane. They drooped with heavy glass icicles. A parade was led by a band blaring out 'Santa Claus is Coming to Town,' followed by Santa driving a sleigh. But Hollywood granted Santa the extra dimension of a Sweetheart and seated beside him was Clara Bow (or was it Mable Normand?) Behind them came a truck with an airplane propeller that showered cornflake 'snow' down on the sexy pair.

One native contribution to the scene appeared everywhere: the poinsettia plant. An entire field of them at the corner of Hollywood and Sunset boulevards disturbed me as being more symbolic of Hollywood than Christmas. But they couldn't disturb a sentimentalist like Wilson. It seemed he'd recently been gifted with a potted poinsettia by a pal named Mousey Miller, who was a shoplifter. 'The little lady heisted it off a counter as Schwab's Drug Store,' said he, 'and I'm a son-of-a-gun if it isn't loaded with Christmas spirit.'

A rash of holiday parties began.

December 21 – Supper Dance at the Selwyns'

Wilson and I found no phony Christmas décor at the Selwyns', nor a single poinsettia. A marquee on the lawn had a ceiling of fresh gardenias; hundreds of them floated on the swimming pool.

The party was in honor of the Selwyns' houseguest, Doris Duke. As an MGM producer, Edgar Selwyn was tied to Culver City, but Ruthie often took flight and covered the capitals of the world with Doris. (Visiting Berlin, Ruthie once wrote on a postcard 'Next week we have a date to meet Mr Hitler.' What a happy world it was when that archfiend could be addressed as 'Mister'!)

Ruth's home was an outpost of international chic. Drawn by the magic of Hollywood were such de-luxe stargazers as the ex-King of Spain; the Cole Porters; the Duke and Duchess of Sutherland; that professional playgirl Elsa Maxwell with Evalyn McLean, owner of the fabulous Hope Diamond, in Elsa's wake to pay the bills; the Princess di Frasso; and her lover, that Crown Prince of the Mafia, Bugsy Siegel, more distinguished looking than any film star until he got murdered.

That night the two richest girls in the world were decorating the scene. Besides Doris, who looked like a Persian princess (and still does), there was Barbara Hutton: a white wraith except for heavy eyebrows that made her seem an Etruscan portrait. She was then the Princess Mdivani, but Barbara's marriages would always be of short duration. Her husbands would find it impossible to save face in the light of Barbara's overpowering publicity; a situation she didn't try to ameliorate. In 1942, when married to Cary Grant, she indulged in the habit of speaking French to her maid, making the world's sexiest husband a silent bystander in his wife's boudoir. Cary couldn't take that humiliation.

The film beauties at that party have faded from my memory, but not our hostess. She caused all the others to seem placid. Ruth's gaiety matched her looks and sometimes Edgar had either to alibi his bride's behavior or else call his marriage quits. He chose the former. 'You see,' explained Edgar, 'Ruth is flirty !'

At a high point in the festivities, Ruth was challenged by Leslie Howard to join him at the other end of the pool, thinking no doubt that she'd jump in and swim the distance. She took the dare but to keep her wispy gown from getting wet and clinging too much, Ruth deftly balanced herself on a floating mat. And then, using her slim white arms as oars, she crossed the pool without getting a drop of water on her dress. One of my most poignant memories of real Hollywood glamour is a vision of that small, slender beauty, prone on a sea of gardenias like a frivolous Ophelia, out-witting Leslie Howard who stood by, hoping she'd fall in and get revealingly doused.

Ruthie was a catalyst. If ever she found a dearth of excitement, she set about supplying it. She once organized a Broadway revue to which all of us contributed material. Neither Ziegfeld nor the Shuberts could have rounded up that roster of talent. But such a high-voltage gaiety was bound to burn itself out. While still young, fresh, and irresistible, Ruthie was felled by t.b. Her death inspired a poem by Rudolf Friml, the famous composer, of which I own a copy and have permission from Ruth's sister, Pansy Schenck, to pass along. Rudi will be forever known for his 'Donkey Serenade' but he could be as eloquent with words as he was with bars of music.

Each star is but
A candle of my faith in
An eternal vow
That those who truly love, walk on
To meet again,
Somewhere, somehow

Sleep love –
No harm can come to thee
Here in my heart, or memory.
Dream love –
That there will come a day
Some peaceful century away
Where we will walk again in Spring
Another world, where children sing.
Angels guard thy star-kissed eyes
Sleep love – sleep love – 'til paradise !

December 24 – Orgy at MGM

The 'orgy' was the annual Christmas party, given to cement morale, break down class distinctions, and keep workers happy throughout the coming year.

Although I had been at the studio less than a week, I'd already found two new cronies: members of the writing staff, Howard Emmett Rogers and John Lee Mahin. As a rule, writers are a bore and never talk about anything but their work; Rogers and Johnny never mentioned it. (Those friendships worked out to be delightfully uncomplicated; Rogers was married to a flaming redhead; an ex-Follies beauty, so attractive she had no urge to be jealous of me. Red was a philosopher. One day, discussing the sexes, she remarked, 'Men may know more than we do, honey, but we girls are smarter!' If I have always been partial to men, it's because there are so few girls like Red Rogers.

Johnny Mahin, tall, brown-haired, and agreeable, was in a constant state of romantic flux. So many fiendish starlets were battling over him, marrying him, divorcing, or suing him that I became a sort of Platonic haven.

The day of the orgy turned out sunny, clear, and hot. Rogers, Johnny, and I first went to the Beverly Hills Derby for lunch with Wilson. We were trying to talk him into going to the party when W. C. Fields toddled in like a rowdy old Santa, tugging a suitcase that gave out the seductive clank of bottles. Wilson preferred to remain with W.C., so we left them to make merry on the contents of W.C.'s suitcase.

Arriving at MGM, we proceeded toward Louis B. Mayer's office and ran smack into the orgy. The entrance to his suite was blocked by a bawdy mob voicing a lot of innuendo. We heard a messenger boy declare libidinous aspirations to Joan Crawford, who fended him off with an arch slap on the wrist.

The situation inside L. B.'s office was a switch on the old *droit du seigneur* in which a VIP was licensed to make a pass at any humble maid. In this case the privilege belonged to secretaries, manicurists, hairdressers, wardrobe girls, and whatnots, who were taking over the boss's lap as if they were starlets.

Presently, Irving wandered through to pay his respects to fun for once in the year. At sight of Irving the girls attacked him en masse. While he was being smeared with lipstick, we moved on toward Arlie's office. There the mob was smaller but no less impetuous. Arlie, as a gourmet, had supplied it with champagne and caviar and, his face frozen into a grin, sat fondling a starlet on each knee – had Arlie been granted a third knee he'd have taken on another. I was willing to be a benign spectator to all this, but Rogers and Johnny had enjoyed too many real adventures to bother with such mild bawdiness, so they suggested we move on to the music department.

Musicians, sensuous by nature, also tend to be uncontrolled, so L. B. had located them out of sight where they couldn't be spotted by the daily guided tours. They occupied a row of sheds at the far end of the back lot, and there we ran into license that was for real. Music was pouring from every sort of sound equipment; office doors were wide open; a number of ladies of the street had been sneaked in through a back entrance. A certain amount of clothing had been discarded and a disheveled Jack Barrymore was offering stardom to a young thing in whose talent he was shamelessly disinterested.

(Once in a while I hear a bawdy joke that is as sound as if it had been worked out by Euclid. That orgy reminded me of this one : It seems a traveling salesman from Cincinnati made a trip to Iran where a certain beautiful Princess picked him up as a curiosity. When our hero got back home he described the adventure to a friend. He told of the Princess's exotic beauty; the palace to which she took him; the vintage wine; the perfumed bath; the hidden violins; the priceless jewels and garments she discarded; and, at last, her shimmering nudity. 'And then what?' our hero's listener gasped. 'Oh, then it was just the same as it is in Cincinnati.')

So much for that Hollywood orgy.

But it was possible for those festivities which we found so innocuous to be accompanied by grim violence. On Christmas Day the obituary columns were lengthened by the activities of drunken drivers who left the studio in droves. That celebration in 1931 was followed by a number of motor crack-ups, some serious but none fatal. However, a carpenter had fallen down a narrow staircase on the outside of a sound stage just as he was calling out the last 'Merry Christmas' of his life.

When I reported the orgy to Mr E. by phone, his psychology, based on clichés, as always made him suspicious of the wrong things. My idea of festivity was to be with Wilson; so Mr E. asked, 'Did you see Gable at the party?' I explained that L. B. had ordered Clark to keep away for fear the girls would tear him limb from limb. At any rate, he was then firmly in the grip of his second wife, Ria Langham, who was rich, refined, ten years older than Clark and in appearance could have been mistaken for his mother.

It would have been pointless to tell my husband that Clark had no more allure for me than the chatty young man who delivered my groceries. Clark was happiest when on camping trips but, like most overly male Americans, he felt required to have a large quota of affairs. Without any thought of being disloyal to a wife or sweetheart, he'd take on any pretty girl who ran after him. Their name, of course, was legion. As a rule they were not outdoor types. Clark's third and fourth wives, Carole Lombard and Sylvia Fairbanks (widow of Douglas), were indoor girls; from both of whom I heard complaints about that canvas sleeping bag of Clark's.

I mostly admired Clark for his lack of vanity. He was equipped with a premature set of false teeth for which he felt no embarrassment. One day I happened on him at an outdoor faucet in the Alley where he'd stopped to wash off his denture. Clark grinned, pointed to his caved-in mouth and said with an exaggerated lisp, 'Look! America's thweet-heart!'

Clark had great luck in his fifth and last marriage to Kay Williams Spreckels, a full-blown American blonde. He left a son, born after Clark died, who from all accounts is already affecting female hearts in the tradition of his daddy. (Contrary to press releases, the boy is not Clark's only child. A short but hectic affair Clark went through with a costar when they were far from Hollywood on location had resulted in the birth of a baby girl. She is now a Park Avenue matron, a dream of beauty like her mamma and married to an important young business executive. I don't know whether she suspects who her father was, but I'm not going to tip her off now.)

Carole Lombard, Clark's third wife, was the wish fulfillment of every man in and out of Hollywood; a natural blonde who, both a lady and a hoyden, had a sense of humor and lack of pretense that seldom go with beauty as glittering as hers. I recall one day when she was strolling down a road and a passing truck driver offered her a lift. Carole accepted and, because the driver was good company, she drove with him all the way to Bakersfield. But before very long the young man began to sense he'd picked up an angel unawares. 'Know something, baby?' he ventured, 'you remind me of Carole Lombard.' 'If you compare me with that cheap floozy, I'll get right off your truck!' Carole flared up. So the driver apologized.

Carole was a truly understanding mate, in a sense that few wives could ever be. Having first been married to William Powell, she understood film stars thoroughly; knew that their status as sex symbols existed largely in the minds of the public – which I'm told is often the case with athletes, prize fighters, and baseball and football idols.

It can now be told that Clark needed assistance in order to live up to his virile appearance and Carole was just the wife to supply it. One day Carole, at a cat party, explained an incident to us girls which came about like this : She had made an acquaintance among the ladies that hung out around the musicians' quarters, one of whom tipped her off to a trade secret which went by the mystifying name of 'Peppermint French.' It required a dime's worth of essence of peppermint which a girl would then use, undiluted, as a mouth wash before a rendezvous with her loved one. Carole carried out instructions and, on entering the boudoir a certain night, found Clark sound asleep. This gave her an idea. Why not add an element of surprise to the innovation of that peppermint? Without waking Clark, she proceeded in a gentle approach which caused her hero, startled by the sudden sting of peppermint, to jump off the bed and sprain his ankle.

Carole always had an antic slant on sex. It never ceased to amuse her. I recall a day when we happened to be on her front porch as one of our higher-class gigolos strode down the street, exercising his lady friend's Pekingese. 'Hi,' called Carole in friendly greeting. 'Hard at work, eh?'

Carole was killed in a plane crash while on a patriotic tour concerning the war effort. The tragic news was phoned to Clark in the middle of the night, when rumor had it he was with another charmer, merely following the normal course of an American male when the little wife is on a trip. It took Carole's death to remind Clark that he'd been unfaithful. He loved her devotedly and must have suffered unbearable guilt. We all felt his enlistment in the Army was an effort to assuage it.

December 29 – Lunch at George Cukor's

I wish I'd mentioned in my datebook some of the guests at that first of George's luncheons I attended, but they must have been formidable. For, as an ace director, George Cukor was, and still is, one of Hollywood's most cultured citizens. His Sunday luncheons have been the nearest thing to a *salon* that ever existed in the movie colony.

One occasion that stands out distinctly is a lunch party he gave to welcome Lady Charles Mendl to the community. Elsie had sold her small palace in Versailles to set up an equally chic household in Benedict Canyon.

Her Ladyship had invented the profession of interior decoration, in which she made use of costly knickknacks, ignoring real works of art or paintings that would pass muster at the Louvre or the Metropolitan Museum. Much of her bric-a-brac, however, was authentic, as was Elsie Mendl herself; a sort of eighteenth-century cockatoo with a voice to match.

Among George's guests on that occasion was Tallulah Bankhead, then making one of her first movies. Tallulah was the foremost naughty girl of her era but, in those days, 'naughty' meant piquant, whereas values have so changed that now, in the 1970s, it generally means nauseating.

Several of us were sitting about George's pool when Elsie Mendl could be heard approaching. Quick as a wink Tallulah slithered out of her dress and by the time Elsie reached us, she was lying on a marble bench, naked except for a bunch of violets which Tallulah held in the pose of Goya's 'Unclothed Maja.' George was furious; Her Ladyship gasped 'Cover yourself at once, you shameless child !' And Tallulah obediently did.

But nudity was not the only shock Tallu provided that day, for violets had been given a bad name by a notorious play called The Captive, in which a bouquet of them was used as communication between two young women who were in love with each other.

Tallu's strip-tease had been motivated by an incident that had recently taken place in Lady Mendl's drawing room. One of her guests remarked that The Captive had been raided in New York and closed by the police. Her Ladyship pretended ignorance of the reason why. 'What is a lesbian ?' she asked, slapping the tea table briskly with a characteristic gesture. 'Tell me what they do !'

Now for years Elsie had had a very close relationship with a Broadway play agent, a lady of width and heft who wore her hair in a crew cut, sported ground-gripper shoes, and was given to shooting her cuffs in a manly gesture. And when Tallu heard Lady Mendl's question, she asked, in her gruff *sotto voce*, 'If Elsie doesn't know what lesbians are, who does?'

December 31 – New Year's Eve with Hearst and Marion

The enormous compound in Santa Monica, which Hearst modestly called the Beach House, was ablaze with lights. It looked like a country club; a main building of 'sea-shore Colonial' and a wide veranda overlooking two swimming pools, one heated, the other at air temperature like certain wines. A tall hedge separated the grounds from the beach, beyond which gleamed the phosphorescent surf of the Pacific. The Hollywood elite was gathered in a ballroom decorated by a collection of portraits; Rembrandts, Van Dykes, Goyas, and Titians. But hanging next to a masterpiece of Goya was a portrait that had been painted by Howard Chandler Christie for the cover of *Cosmopolitan* magazine, and showed Marion in the cute boy's outfit she wore in *Little Old New York*.

Dear slap-happy Marion was the gayest of hostesses. Hearst, himself a teetotaler, gave strict orders to his entourage that Marion must follow his example. On festive occasions, however, he did allow champagne to be served and this, in addition to his duties as host, made it difficult to keep tabs on his loved one. Furthermore, Marion could handle liquor in her youth; it only increased her capacity for fun.

I've known very few stars to be unimpressed by their stardom. Marion valued her career largely because she felt it overcame the blight of being a 'kept girl.' I never realized her feelings on that subject until one day when I happened to suggest that Mr E. and I could pick her up and take her with us to a certain party. 'I'm n-n-not going.' 'But why not?' 'Everybody will be there.' I then heard a fact I'd never before realized; Marion attended very few parties outside her own home, where she felt guests wouldn't walk out on her as a 'fallen woman.' 'You see N-N-Nita, when I get among st-st-strangers I never know . . .'

On the part of W. R., Marion's stardom was a matter of personal vanity. He wanted the whole world to witness the treasure he possessed in Marion. He never wearied of sitting alone in his projection room, running those movies again and again, gloating over every pretty close-up.

The Charleston W. R. danced with Marion on New Year's Eve was as spry as a teen-age Mickey Rooney's; like many people of bulk, W. R. was extremely light on his feet.

Milling about the ballroom with Wilson, I was stopped by Irene Castle, recently arrived from Paris. She approved my gingham ball gown that had been so audaciously trimmed in sable by Mainbocher. She tousled my tomboy bob. 'I see you've taken my advice and kept away from hairdressers!' said Irene.

Another supersophisticated guest was a British Duchess. I don't recall her name, but she was genial, plump, and nonetheless imposing in a rather alarmingly deep décoleté. Marion had previously told me the Duchess posed a problem in etiquette. At supper she would naturally occupy the place of honor to the right of W. R., but what other Hollywood executive was sufficiently distingué to sit at the other side of a Duchess? Finally W. R. settled for 'Gentleman Jack' Warner as being the glass of fashion and mold of Hollywood form.

When supper ended, it came time for W. R. to toast his guest of honor. But the Duchess, in bowing acknowledgement, caused her décolleté to slip without her realizing it and there bounced into full view a very robust *poitrine*. We all sat frigid with alarm. W. R., having ordered the orchestra to follow his toast with the British anthem, dazedly signaled it to start. And then Gentleman Jack rose to the occasion. His voice ringing out above 'God Save the King,' he sounded the alert. 'Hey, Duchess! Your tit's out!'

The Duchess blushed a deep crimson and popped herself back into her bodice, but being a lady born and bred, she herself led an uproar of laughter.

Hollywood may have been uncouth, but from being the remote outpost it was at the beginning, it was now in the mainstream of life. Any number of friends I'd made elsewhere – in New York, Paris, London, and Berlin – were now permanent residents of Hollywood. Other friends, like Mencken and H. G. Wells, could be counted on for visits. Most enthralling of all was the fact that a day seldom passed when I didn't see Wilson, or the two of us would spend our late hours with Lionel or Jack Barrymore, W. C. Fields, or Gene Fowler, a group with as much *élan* as the clique I'd left behind me in New York.

Picking up my datebook for 1932, I leafed through it and my heart stopped cold at June 15. It was the day my contract would end and all the fun would be over.

I tried not even to think of going back to being a satellite of Mr E., whose course was one perpetual dead end. Then, one morning as I was crossing the Alley near Irving's office, Sam Marx, the head of the script department, stopped to say, 'Irving asked me to tell you he's pleased with your work.' Then, in the manner of an afterthought, he added, 'By the way, he'd like to keep you here *on a permanent basis.*' As I tried to stop my heart from skipping more than a beat or two, Sam continued, 'But our maximum salary for long-term contracts is twenty-five hundred a week. Would you agree to sign for two years at that rate?'

In a state of euphoria I accepted Irving's deal right then and there. It meant that my good times would be assured for two more years, while Mr E. could remain in New York nursing his ailments and basking in the sympathy of his current lady friend. I hurried to phone him the great news.

But to my surprise, Mr E. was alarmed. 'You haven't *signed* that deal, have you?' 'Why no, it was only brought up this morning in the Alley.' 'Good!' he exclaimed. 'But don't talk business to just anyone, Buggie dear. This matter has got to be handled by an agent!' 'No, no, darling!' I protested. 'This is between Irving and me and he's my friend!'

'Look, Buggie, in the movie business nobody's a friend. A good agent will be able to arrange a deal for *the two of us to work together again as a team.*'

I listened, stunned by a proposal that would forever end my fun. I remembered back to the old Doug Fairbanks days when Mr E.'s 'collaboration' consisted of glancing over my morning's work while he was eating breakfast in bed. From time to time he'd say, 'But, Buggie, *this will never do!*' 'What's wrong, Mr E.?' Shaking his head in despair he'd answer, 'You've left out another comma, as usual!'

Those sessions took a lot of pleasure out of my daily life. I could only hope and pray that Irving would refuse us as a team. But, alas, Irving let me down. Always ready to take a gamble on a writer, he offered Mr E. a six-month contract at $1000 a week.

Disappointed as Mr E. was over a short term and a salary less than his Buggie's, he phoned to tell me he'd accepted

Irving's offer. And, with a show of self-confidence I could only find pathetic, he added, 'At least it will give me a toe hold until Thalberg recognizes my value.' I had no illusions about Mr E.'s 'value'; I shuddered at the thought of him in conference with a sharp mind like Irving's. Mr E. was given to repeating himself or mistaking the subject at hand and gibing in with some completely foreign matter.

I tried to put up an argument and said, 'Stay in New York, darling, where your doctors can look after you. Working at the studio would be much too hectic.'

'Don't you want me out there?' he asked mournfully. I answered with the required lie and, to cover my guilt, even offered to find him an apartment.

And then, although his voice took on a honeyed tone, Mr E. dropped a bombshell. 'Buggie dear, don't you think we ought to give our marriage another try?'

For a while I was too appalled to answer.

Living alone in a cozy bungalow with a Persian cat and a competent maid to bully me, I was happier than I had ever been. The separate lives we'd led had been pleasant for Mr E., too. And handling my money gave him an occupation that saved his face.

But while I was stalling for time, Mr E. came clean. 'Let's face it, Buggie, Thalberg only made me that offer *as your husband.*'

Had Mr E. repeated his old cliché that he lived only for his little Bug, I might have argued further. But he had admitted to skulduggery with something like bravado. So as the spineless pushover I will always be, I accepted my husband's proposal.

Almost instantly I had a foretaste of what life would be like with Mr E. On our very first evening together, I sat fondling my cat when Mr E. spoke up. 'Buggie dear, do you mind getting rid of that animal?'

I loved my cat and asked why.

'You know I hate pets. I've never owned one.'

That edict was taken as a personal insult by my maid, Marianne. 'If Emperor goes, then I go too!'

Marianne was free to go but I was stuck. So I gave Emperor to Marianne and they went off into the night together, taking a great deal of charm with them.

7

I Got What I Wanted

EVEN before we were married Mr E. had already put into practice many of the thrills a masochistic bride could desire. I had become Mr E.'s collaborator-helpmeet-errand girl-sweetheart and traveling companion. Seldom was a Hollywood union as secure; with so many ties to bind us, our marriage would go on forever.

But, back in 1926, my opportunities for service had been further increased, for I was able to take on the duties of a practical nurse. Mr E. had been stricken with a dread form of laryngitis that prevented him speaking above a whisper. Following the instructions of his throat specialist, I applied ice packs and hot fomentations, sprayed his throat, regulated his diet, and provided him with massage. But, for all my ministrations, Mr E.'s voice only got weaker and, without daring to breathe the awful word, I began to think of ... cancer.

Finally Mr E. was advised to see America's foremost throat specialist, Dr Chevalier Jackson. He lived in Philadelphia and we drove down from New York to see him. Dr Jackson, a benign old autocrat, asked for time to study Mr E.'s collection of reports and X-rays, but as we were leaving his office, a nurse quietly called me back and informed me I was to return in an hour *without letting my husband know of it.* I kept that appointment in an agony of fear. The doctor began by saying it was urgent for me to know the truth about my husband and as I turned rigid with fright, he added, 'There's nothing at all wrong with his throat. His loss of voice is the result of some sort of neurosis that can only be brought to light through psychotherapy.'

In my relief that the disease was only in Mr E.'s mind, my first reaction was to underestimate it, but the doctor put me right on that score. He warned me that such a patient generally resented being a *malade imaginaire* and a cure might demand years of psychiatric treatment. In spite of Dr Jackson's warning, I left his office in a glow of hope. There was nothing wrong with my precious charge that would even require an aspirin.

When Dr Jackson brought up the subject of psychiatry the next day, Mr E. was inclined to be resentful, but he finally agreed to consult one of the best of the New York specialists, Dr Jelliffe. A few sessions with Dr Jelliffe in New York bored Mr E. as being too theoretical and he deserted psychiatry for a realist who was treating the golden throat of the great Caruso.

And then an incident occurred which brought me together socially with Dr Jelliffe. He phoned to ask if he might bring a friend to tea and added, rather strangely, that he preferred they see me alone, without my husband.

Dr Jelliffe's companion turned out to be an English confrere who was in New York attending a medical convention. He was Court physician to George V and had brought a message to me from the King. It seemed that in bidding his royal patient good-by, the doctor asked if he could do anything for His Majesty in America. The King replied that he might look up the author of *Gentlemen Prefer Blondes* and tell her that the Prince of Wales had bought nineteen copies of the book and that the entire royal family found it very 'laughable.' I considered this pretty tolerant of them, in view of the fun I'd poked at the Prince's horsemanship and his mother's cast-iron bonnets.

After the British doctor left that afternoon, Dr Jelliffe lingered on to explain why he'd wanted to see me alone. It was because Mr E. might have suffered a serious relapse on hearing those compliments from British royalty.

As I listened dumbfounded, Dr Jelliffe went on to inform me the specific reason for Mr E.'s loss of voice. The poor man, suffering agonies over the success of *Gentlemen Prefer Blondes*, had invented a disease as a means of attracting attention.

Dr Jelliffe proceeded to quote from H. L. Mencken that a husband may survive the fact of a wife *having* more money than he, but if she *earns* more, it can destroy his very essence.

Overcome with guilt that I, myself, was the cause of Mr E.'s distress, I asked how I could undo the harm I'd done. 'The only possible cure for your husband,' answered Dr Jelliffe, 'is to give up your career.'

Nothing could have been easier. We had no need for money, and, although I enjoyed writing as a pastime, I never had much respect for female scribblers, least of all myself. But a publisher had already coerced me into starting a sequel to be called *But Gentlemen Marry Brunettes*. I resolved to finish the book as quickly as possible, after which Mr E. would be through forever with any jealousy of my career.

Even before my first book came out, however, I had gained a certain amount of attention as a writer. On a first visit to Paris in 1923, it amazed me to be interviewed and quoted because I'd written scripts for Douglas Fairbanks. It was his overwhelming vogue in silent movies that gave me a first hint that films were emerging into sophistication. In time fashionable Parisians would be sporting dark glasses in fog, mist, and rain because Doug Fairbanks wore them to protect him from the glaring California sun. The most elegant Paris couturiers would start padding women's sleeves because of the preternatural width of Joan Crawford's shoulders.

At a cocktail party one day I met a distinguished Scandinavian professor, a psychologist who remarked that Hollywood was making a great contribution to world culture. 'Culture?' I spoke up. 'Are you joking?'

'Not in the least, young lady. Hollywood is rejuvenating the spirits of a tired old civilization. Its jaunty film plots are sweeping aside the moldy problems of Ibsen, Tolstoi, and Dostoevski ... getting us back to basic simplicity. Hollywood has given culture a fresh start. Who knows how far it will go, as the movies emerge from their infancy?'

I couldn't entirely agree with the old professor as regards Hollywood culture. I remembered back to when, as a little girl, my hero of Romance had been the youthful King of Spain, Alfonso. But (although he had been demoted and became an ex-king) Alfonso had recently been the house-guest of Doug Fairbanks. And when Doug had asked him if there was any particular film star His Majesty wanted to meet, he eagerly answered, 'Fatty Arbuckle.'

Fatty! Who had lost caste even in Hollywood because he brought about the death of gay little Virginia Rappe while she was trying to fight off his unorthodox love-making. But when Doug mentioned that scandal to Alfonso, he remarked, 'How unfair! Why it might have happened to any of us.'

I couldn't see much culture where a king wanted to associate with Fatty Arbuckle.

'When are you going back to Hollywood?' the professor had asked me.

'Never.'

'Never? You're not going to write any more movies?'

'No.'

'But why not?'

I stretched to my full four feet eleven and stated proudly, 'Because I'm a married woman, Professor! My husband needs me!'

The very vehemence of that boast might have indicated I was ceasing to be needed. During the spring of 1926 Mr E. had promised to show me London for the first time. But a few days before our scheduled departure on a Cunard liner, he suddenly found a reason that kept him in New York. He urged me to leave without him, promising to join me later. Disappointed and unused to traveling without him, I had sailed for England accompanied by a French maid who was my age and had the same heft of ninety pounds. We must have seemed two rather undistinguished little creatures when we checked in at the Savoy Hotel in London.

The next morning I ventured into the Strand, feeling diffident over being alone in a strange city. The Strand was seething with noise and confusion; then presently, to my bewilderment, I began to be aware that I, myself, was contributing to the hubbub. News vendors all along the way were barking out the headlines on the small posters which are so typical of a London street scene, and they carried my name in red and black lettering: 'Anita Loos in London.'

As I listened to those cockney voices I was chilled by that new danger to my marriage. What if Mr E. were there to hear his Buggie's name being called out in the London street?

I sought refuge from that thought by going back to the hotel. By that time the phones in both my rooms were ringing. While I answered one, my maid tried to cope with the other but, speaking only French, she added to the confusion. And from that time on, day and night, my phones never stopped ringing.

The British are prone to magnify writers. They pampered Noel Coward, Michael Arlen, Freddy Lonsdale, and Somerset

Maugham as if they were matinee idols. And interest in me was heightened by the fact that I'd once lived in the magical world of D. W. Griffith, Douglas Fairbanks, Charlie Chaplin, and Mary Pickford.

Invitations began pouring in from the kind of men I'd dreamed of meeting from the time I was a girl; H. G. Wells, Arnold Bennett, Lytton Strachey. But they didn't quite blot out the fact that Mr E. had set me adrift alone in London.

There were also disturbances, in the form of cranks.

One morning I was getting dressed for lunch at the home of Lady Colefax, London's indefatigable lion huntress, when there was a disturbing interruption from a character who had been phoning me several times a day. With an excess of British nonconformity he had been making headlines by hiding under the bushes in Hyde Park, naked except for a coating of burnt cork, and then jumping into view when solitary females happened by.

He would begin with some perfectly aimless comment, from which he would launch into obscenities that would do credit to a best-selling novel of the Seventies. I had never even heard such characters existed, and the fact that my tormentor spoke cultured English made him all the more alarming.

I might have refused to answer phone calls except that I was frantic to hear from Mr E. in New York. It had been several days since he'd called and, when I tried to phone him, he was off somewhere on a motor trip. So I hoped against hope that he hadn't heard about my adventures in London. But when a call finally came through first thing he said was, 'Well, Buggie, how does it feel to be famous?'

His tone was only mildly sarcastic but I could think of no other answer than to burst into tears and slam down the receiver. Forgetting all about Lady Colefax's luncheon, I just lay sobbing on the chaise longue and let the phone ring on and on. It might have been Mr E. calling back, but to what purpose?

A chilling fear gripped my heart that my cherished Mr E. was drifting away; I was about to lose the chief reason I'd yet found for living.

8

But Did I Want It?

WHILE Mr E. remained in New York, I carried a smoldering torch for him all over London. But one afternoon I was lunching in the grill of the Savoy Hotel with a beautiful blonde member of London's 'Bright Young People,' as the swingers of that day were called. She had probably picked me up as a sort of conversation piece. Presently, our table was approached by a gentleman of enormous distinction who begged pardon for the intrusion and introduced himself. He was Viscount D'Abernon.

Then in his sixties, Lord D'Abernon bore a marked resemblance to Edward VII. It seemed obvious that he was attracted by my dazzling companion, until he fixed his attention on me and asked, 'Am I right in thinking that you're Miss Loos?' When I enquired how he came to recognize me, His Lordship said, 'I've always felt that if I happened to be anywhere in your vicinity, I'd know you!' *Boom!* Just like that !

The statement was dramatic enough to shake up any brunette, even though it needn't have taken extrasensory perception for me to be spotted; my photos had been around in a number of magazines. At any rate, His Lordship had responded to those jokes I'd written with all the ardor of a Robert Browning to the highfalutin poems of Elizabeth Barrett . . . sex at its most cerebral.

Disregarding my blonde friend, Lord D'Abernon invited me for lunch next day and from then on we lunched together several times a week at all the glamour spots of London; Claridge's, Quaglino's, and Boulestan's.

We went to concerts, museums, and galleries, where I came increasingly to appreciate His Lordship's eminence. As a trustee of the Tate Gallery, Lord D'Abernon was not required to check his walking stick at the entrance as ordinary mortals do and when he brandished his cane to point out details in a painting, it impressed me no end, a fact of which I'm sure he was aware.

Although Lord D'Abernon never spoke of his personal life, I learned about it from others. He had first come into prominence in 1883 when he was appointed President of the Council on Ottoman Public Debt at Constantinople. Dealing with Turks is a circuitous business and the youthful diplomat was a great success at outsmarting them. Following World War I, he was appointed Ambassador to Germany and entrusted with the tricky job of helping put the Versailles Treaty into work. He had now retired and was writing a memoir about his postwar activities in Berlin.

In his youth, D'Abernon had married a young beauty of the Edwardian Court, when it was the world center of glamour and gaiety, just as Hollywood was now. But Lady D'Abernon involved in his diplomatic career and Lady ties, the two had drifted into a vague relationship with D'Abernon involved in his diplomatic career and Lady D'Abernon an important hostess at their town house in Portland Place and at their country estate, Esher.

Ultimately the even tenor of their lives was disrupted by a terrible accident; a fire in which Lady D'Abernon's beauty, in those days before plastic surgery, was scarred beyond any hope of being restored. From that time on she never appeared in public; even at home she hid her face behind a black veil. She lived in complete seclusion at Esher and D'Abernon never mentioned her to me.

Lord D'Abernon provided me with a social life that made even Hollywood appear colorless. To me, London seemed to be populated by characters who behaved as if eccentricity were normal; but, unlike Hollywood, London wasn't self-conscious about it; everything was cozy. The great London hostess, Emerald Cunard, outdid Mae Murray in wearing wacky get-ups, but they were a sign of Her Ladyship's *strength* of character, not the lack of it, as with our stupid little Mae.

The first time Lord D'Abernon led me into the drawing room of Lady Ottoline Morrell, she was standing beside the portrait of Lytton Strachey by Augustus John, done when both the painter and his subject were unknown. Her Ladyship, like Gertrude Stein in Paris, discovered important new painters before they were acclaimed by critics. But, unlike the able-bodied Gertrude, Lady Ottoline was a fragile beauty who seemed to be floating in a cloud of pink chiffon.

Her Ladyship was kindness itself. She took the trouble to send me a note Strachey wrote her, in which he mentioned me as 'the divine A.' I knew he wrote those words with tongue in cheek, but it was a warm and friendly condescension, the same sort that later caused Cecil Beaton to describe me in his *Book of Beauty* as 'the quintessence of cuteness.'

D'Abernon and I became fixture at the lunch parties of Lady Colefax. Sybil never ceased to chase after celebrities; her Rolls-Royce was equipped with a small desk on which she wrote fan letters. But her handwriting looked like a collection of primitive fishhooks and never made any sense.

Sybil had a rival hostess in Syrie Maugham, who was the inventor, along with our Brooklynite, Lady Mendl, of a brand new racket: interior decoration. She had done away with pompous Edwardian décor, replacing plush with chintz, duplicating the window blinds of ancient Venice, and treating everything to a coat of white paint. The homes of Sybil and Syrie were close to each other in the Chelsea district and so bright that on a sunny day there was small difference between the gardens and the indoors.

Syrie Maugham was then in the first round of a lifelong battle with the famous author whom she had just divorced. Never known for her reticence, Syrie's conversation dealt with the awful things Somerset Maugham was doing to her; in fact some of his finest talent went into the invention of diabolic things to do to Syrie. He found ways to flaunt her successor, who was of the wrong sex to rationalize any woman's jealousy. Syrie's life was as packed with heady emotion as any that Maugham ever achieved on his typewriter.

Luncheon parties were rather short; by two-thirty they ended as abruptly as they began; one left with an elation that continued until teatime when the gossip and excitement began all over again.

Sometimes, although not often, I inveigled Lord D'Abernon into the theatrical world where I belonged and he was a stranger. One such affair was a charity garden party which was graced by the Prince of Wales and a team of young American entertainers, Vivian and Rosetta Duncan. The sisters were typical show-business cut-ups, famous for their burlesque version of *Uncle Tom's Cabin*, which was then playing to packed houses in London. The Duncan girls were introduced to the Prince of Wales and, while bantering with him, Rosetta asked a riddle: 'What is it that everybody in the Kingdom can see, except the King?' His Highness suggested that the answer might be 'his equal'; but in Rosetta's version, the answer was 'a joke.' I repeated Rosetta's quip to D'Abernon and it delighted him. But actually his interest in my lively friends was more intellectual than active; so I generally made the nightly rounds with younger escorts and reported them to His Lordship at lunch or tea next day.

At that time London swung without being self-conscious about it, as in the Sixties. The theatrical set was dominated by Ivor Novello, the musical-comedy star. Ivor was so beautiful he might have posed for Donatello as the youthful David. He was also competent to write the books, lyrics, and melodies of the romantic shows in which he starred. The youth of London sighed over Ivor with the same ardor that they scream in ecstasy today over exponents of diabolism like Mick Jagger. Ivor's productions were easy to forget, but he wrote a marching song for World War I, 'Keep the Home Fires Burning,' that will be sung as long as soldiers go away to war.

Almost every night after the theater Ivor and his fun-loving mother received fellow artists, among them Noel Coward, Gertie Lawrence, and Bea Lillie, a trio just emerging into fame. The excitement of going to Ivor's began with a ride in a rickety lift so small that London's favorite fat boy, Henry Sherek, had to climb the stairs. (Today, Ivor's apartment has been taken over by business offices but a brass plaque on the door serves to commemorate the glamour of its past.)

One of London's most fashionable hostesses was the dashing Mrs Jean Norton, who enjoyed the attentions of the Prince of Wales and was one of several precursors of the young American who was later to become the Duchess of Windsor. Mrs Norton frequently entertained in her town house, inviting Americans of whom His Highness was particularly fond; among them Fred and Adele Astaire and George Gershwin. We used to hang over Jean Norton's piano half the night, listening to George improvise. But through it all I would be preoccupied: Where are *you*, Mr E.? I'd be mentally asking.

79

Fred Astaire gave lessons in tap dancing to the Prince of Wales. His Highness sneaked Fred into the palace through a side doorway; nobody was supposed to know that Fred had ordered his august pupil a pair of dance shoes fitted with metal tips for tapping.

Adele's situation in London was unique; wherever she went, in the street or theater lobbies, Dellie was besieged by fans for whom she was always happy to oblige with a few Charleston steps; a procedure which irked the self-effacing Fred. One of Dellie's great amusements was, and still is, to shock her tremendously correct brother.

It soon became understood that Lord D'Abernon would come to tea every day in my sitting room overlooking the Thames at the Savoy. I realized that this was a hazard and waited in trepidation for 'the pass' that sooner or later was sure to come.

I began to wonder what form it might take with such an elegant and cultured Englishman. In Hollywood, 'the pass' generally started off by kidding-on-the-square. And if a girl encouraged the joke, it segued into action. Sometimes the pass took the crude form of a lunge without any dialogue at all. But the classical Hollywood pass, as immortalized by D. W. Griffith, pictured a weightless little girl, like Lillian Gish, being chased around the furniture by an overpowering sophisticate. So that was more or less what I came to expect from my august suitor.

In those cozy sessions at my tea table, His Lordship frequently mentioned subjects that edged precariously on sex. As a child in Germany, he had been exposed to the clique that surrounded Richard Wagner and he declared that I resembled Wagner's beloved Cosima. It was a safe compliment because who among my set knew what Cosima looked like? I felt he'd brought her up in order to introduce the subject of a love affair; *any* love affair.

At the same time he never ran out of safe but lively conversation. D'Abernon had been Gentleman in Waiting to King George, and, talking out of turn, he used to brief me about his life at Court. His affection for the royal family was warmed by his amusement over their all-too-prosaic whims. At one time the aged and exquisite Dowager Queen Alexandra went through a schoolgirl crush on a cowboy star of American films named Eddy Polo.

'Do you know Mr Polo?' His Lordship asked me.

'*Know* him? Why even in Hollywood nobody knows Eddy Polo. His pictures are what we call "Grade B Westerns." They're manufactured for moviehouses in slum areas. Where would Queen Alexandra ever have seen Eddy Polo?'

Well – see him she had, and she immediately placed an order with a London film exchange for every Eddy Polo movie to be rushed to the palace the moment it arrived.

'Now I've heard everything!' I told His Lordship.

D'Abernon shook his head. 'How little you appreciate Hollywood, dear child! Her daydreams about that movie actor have helped to recompense a very beautiful lady for all of Edward the Seventh's infidelities.'

(I had once seen Queen Alexandra in a newsreel. She was in Hyde Park taking the air in a motor brougham which looked archaic enough to have been a carriage. She was slender and dressed with much more chic than royalty had any need for. Like Isak Dinesen and Alice Longworth, Alexandra in her eighties possessed a charisma that actually amounted to sex appeal. Eddy Polo would have flipped for Queen Alexandra, just as she had flipped for him. Romances like that are what have given Hollywood its true value.)

Another of my beau's stories indicated that the hearts of the royal family beat in rhythm with the hearts of Hollywood. Queen Mary, in her adoration of publicity, could have vied with any movie star.

At the time of Rudolph Valentino's death in New York one past-mistress of publicity had announced that Rudy was her fiancé. She forthwith boarded the Santa Fe in Los Angeles and rushed to his bier, fainting in front of cameras all the way to New York. Only his intimates knew that Rudy was having a torrid romance with one of my girl friends which had to be kept secret because she was married to a French count. So the ruse worked out well for all concerned ... Rudy's self-styled fiancée got her publicity and the scandal, which might have harmed the young Countess, remained a secret.

At any rate, whenever Queen Mary graced a public gathering, she immediately looked for the photographers and, if none was in evidence, she'd tap her parasol and complain, 'I see no cameras! Where are the cameras?'

Queen Mary's relationship with King George was as cozy as if they belonged in Upper Tooting. D'Abernon had been on one of the royal progresses when the Queen, as was her custom, immediately went to inspect the sleeping arrangements. When she saw that their bedroom was equipped with twin beds, she took it as a flagrant lese majesty; one that caused a hasty scramble to find an old-fashioned double bed.

I asked D'Abernon if their existence didn't get monotonous. 'Not in the least! It is permeated with romantic intimacies; they conjure up fond nicknames, such as "Bobo," "Bubu," "Boysie," and "Cissy."' (Again like Hollywood, where Louella Parsons, our Queen of Nullity, was affectionately called 'Lolly.')

One of the reigning family's most sentimental comradeships was between King George and his girlish daughter-in-law, the present Dowager Queen Elizabeth. D'Abernon told me that the two spent the cocktail hour giggling together and that they sauntered in to dinner, arm in arm, like sweethearts.

Well – the long expected 'pass' finally transpired. It was on a misty day of London fog when His Lordship and I were in my hotel suite with the entire space of a settee between us. Without any build-up at all, I was politely asked, 'Would it please you for us to retire to your other room?'

The 'other room,' of course, contained a bed. Still under the thrall of Mr E., it took a long moment to gather the courage to answer, 'I'd rather not, Your Lordship.'

'As you wish, my dear. I shan't bring the matter up again.'

The whole affair was so restrained that Hollywood wouldn't have wasted one frame of film on it. Nevertheless, thought I : Now I've put an end to this romance !

I couldn't have been more wrong, for I was about to learn an answer to that great Shakespearean riddle. 'Tell me where is fancy bred, / Or in the heart or in the head?'

9

Sex without Bravado

In Hollywood a brush-off such as I'd given Lord D'Abernon would have been followed by those concerned becoming mortal enemies. It bewildered me that His Lordship behaved as if nothing had ever happened.

And, under his aegis, I made friends whose influences have remained with me always. One of them was Margot Asquith. Her husband had been Prime Minister of Great Britain from 1908 to 1916 and his services to the Crown had earned him the title of Earl of Oxford. But so penetrating was Margot's native strain that her identity as an Asquith far outshone that of the Countess of Oxford. At first sight, Margot seemed much too frail and slender to keep up her hectic social life. But on the subject of weight she gave me a bit of advice I've always remembered. 'Never get fat, dear child. Fat smothers anybody's vitality.'

At parties, Margot always included me in the family group that huddled about her, too greedy of each other's company to bear a moment's separation. (In D'Abernon's memoirs he said of them : 'The Asquiths exceed any group in England for conversational momentum.' But he added, 'The intention of most people in society is to shine, not to be shone upon.')

Margot's favorite in her family was her son 'Puffin' (none but strangers ever called him Antony). Puffin bore evidence to the extent that London was Hollywoodized : he was soon planning to go there and learn to direct films.

Margot Asquith was considered to be coldly cynical, but after her husband's death she wrote me a letter that gives quite another picture of her.

44 Bedford Square
June 14, 1928
5:30 a.m.

Dearest Anita,

It is so difficult to say all one feels in a short space. Just now I am always afraid of crying or breaking down. I never sleep, as you see by the hour I am writing. I am horribly lonely except when Puff and I are together.

The architecture of my life has been shattered, and were it not for Puff there is no reason for me. Your sympathy, intelligence, simplicity and, above all, human understanding have been very healing.

Goodbye. Do not forget your

Loving Margot Asquith

It seemed incredible that a woman of Margot's culture would open her heart to an unschooled little American who was younger than she by two generations. But then the same had been true of Lord D'Abernon. I began to lose a feeling of dependence on Mr E. for my identity.

(The Asquiths I knew are gone now. But just before Puffin was stricken with the ailment of which he died four months later, he invited Lillian Gish and me to visit him in Rome, where he was preparing to direct a film. *The Shoes of the Fisherman.* Lillian and I accepted, but we were only playing a little game; actually all three of us were too civilized to get together in the tarantula nest of a Roman movie studio. Just before Puffin died in London, I was in New York and we said good-by over the telephone.)

In 1926 Mr E. steeled himself to join me in London, and I was apprehensive about how he'd accept D'Abernon. According to the London way of life, there was no reason why I shouldn't go on seeing him daily as usual. But still the problem rankled. It was the first time I'd be faced with marital jealousy. True, I had many men friends who liked me because we laughed at the same jokes. But D'Abernon's feelings were obviously not those of a pal.

Mr E. first met D'Abernon at tea where there were plenty of casual things to talk about; but from time to time I'd notice Mr E. gazing at me with a peculiar new look; as if he'd never seen me before or, even more disturbing, as if I were some sort of curio. It was eerie, but like most awful moments in life, it didn't last very long and I was soon able to forget it.

At the same time Mr E. actually began to be diverted by a few incidents which concerned his Bug.

Most Londoners took it for granted that my novel was an autobiography. Every time I was introduced to strangers, they reacted in surprise that I was not a blonde with a long history of scandal behind me. They would never have believed that I learned about gentlemen's preferences through being a brunette.

One of those misunderstandings concerned a certain Mr Cochran, who was the manager of our hotel. One day I had asked him if he'd supply me with a small clock for my bedroom. When, after several days, no clock arrived I told my maid to phone Mr Cochran and remind him of his promise. She forthwith took my address book and found the name of Alexander Cochran, the distinguished theatrical impresario. She then put through a call to his home and, he being out, announced to Mrs Cochran that her husband had promised a bedroom clock to Miss Loos and would she kindly see that he made good on it. Later, my maid reported having told Mr Cochran's wife of his promise but still no clock arrived. So my maid kept right on phoning Mrs Cochran.

Presently, I began to note a certain chill in the behavior of Mrs Cochran when I happened to meet her at parties. Eventually Alex called me up, utterly baffled by a jealous scene he'd gone through with his wife, in which she accused him of having bought me a 'jeweled' clock for my bedroom. 'Could I possibly clear up the mystery?' Alex asked. I could and did, to the relief of them both, and the amusement of us all.

The episode, moreover, gave Mr E. something to dine out on. Hopefully, he was beginning to take our situation in stride. Furthermore, he began to find a life of his own in London. As the President of the Actors' Equity Association, there were labor problems for him to discuss with the British Actors' Association.

Finally, a time came when Mr E. was invited to make a speech before the German Actors' Association. So we left London for Berlin, with a tour of Germany to follow. It would mean good-by to D'Abernon and any possible complications.

In Berlin, Mr E. was vastly cheered at his acclaim by the theatrical set; but even more so by a humiliation that was accorded his Buggie one day. He was introduced to a large audience of German actors by an earnest, bosomy character actress who said, in effect, 'It is an honor to greet such an eminent American as Herr Emerson. He is helping our nation to forget the insults of another American who has cast abominable aspersions at us. I refer, of course, to the woman who wrote that distasteful book, *Blondinin Bevorzugt*.'

Nobody in the audience knew that the distasteful authoress was none other than Frau Emerson, who was sitting meekly in their midst. So the laugh could only be shared by Mr E. and me. Again, as in London, Mr E. took to dining out on that joke and it became another pleasant bond between us.

One day, just before we were to start for Salzburg, Mr E. came across a letter D'Abernon had written me which stated : 'Remember you are a very precious possession to a dull world. You have become, in your eagle's nest, a part of London. I'm very anxious to see as much of you as possible. It would be a great joy to see you in Salzburg; to enjoy your sharp and penetrating causticity' (a word I had to look up in the dictionary. My suitor was always giving me credit for qualities that existed in his own mind). 'There is no one as acute and as free from all nonsense,' his letter continued. 'In this muddling age it is a relief and an exhilaration.'

Admitting that he'd read D'Abernon's letter, Mr E. suggested, 'Why don't you invite the old boy to join us in Salzburg?'

Was Mr E. beginning to gain in self-assurance? Well — time perhaps would tell.

D'Abernon joined us and we became, in short, a ménage à trois, with none of the messy complications of sex.

One of the locations to which D'Abernon followed us was the little Bavarian village of Berchtesgaden. In those days just before Hitler's rise to prominence, it was merely a spa where fat Germans went to lose weight. I'd heard about the cure and, weighing in at ninety-six pounds over a normal ninety, remembered Margot Asquith's advice.

We lived in Berchtesgaden's luxury hotel, which boasted heavy-handed, German scarlet-and-gold décor. But a really authentic grandeur was contributed by the view through large windows of a mountain crag that loomed above the village.

It was in Berchtesgaden that a miserable, undersized Viennese house painter with a diabolic inferiority complex showed up, and among the daydreams that infested his rickety mind was one in which he saw himself as the god of a fortress on the top of that butte. Well – he attained his goal, as people always do when they dream with over-powering intensity. But if it is violent enough to destroy the equilibrium of an entire world, it would be better to take sleeping pills, *nicht wahr?*

I soon lost my extra pounds in a bathtub filled with sizzling foam. The Kuranstalt still exists for any *leichtfertig Amerikaner* who overdramatizes a gain of six pounds.

(After Lord D'Abernon completed the first volume of his memoirs, he asked me to read the manuscript and give him my suggestions. It was ridiculous that at my age and ignorance of world affairs, my criticism could have had any possible value. However, I did recommend a more dramatic arrangement of some of the chapters and, when the book came out in 1928, D'Abernon wrote me : 'Thanks to your revision, *An Ambassador of Peace* got tremendous write-ups in the press, much more than I expected, or than it deserves.'

When I received my copy of the book, I found that the printed dedication was to 'The fairest of critics,' and his cryptic use of the adjective 'fair' was meant for me alone.)

Sometimes His Lordship offered me any amount of loot I might care to garner; once he wrote from Paris, 'I shall be here 'til Wednesday, so let me know if there's any shopping you wish carried out.' But, as a true brunette, I never suggested a thing.

Later on, in Munich the two of us found we had a mutual fondness for the paintings of Cranach the Elder. I had dis-covered that painter in Paris and had even tried to buy a small Cranach engraving I'd found at the bargain price of $4000. But when I dragged Mr E. to the gallery and begged him for the money, I was given a lecture instead : 'A work of art should never be owned by an individual. It is the rightful property of a museum, where the entire public can enjoy it.'

I still wanted that engraving terribly and the fact that we had stepped out of the gallery into a downpour of rain didn't serve to brighten my spirits, even though Mr E. did his best. 'Just consider, Buggie dear, that people who buy expensive pictures are only showing off!' At which he stepped into his new custom-built Rolls-Royce and whizzed off to keep an appointment, leaving me to try and find a taxi in the rain. I didn't know which was worse, catching pneumonia or losing my Cranach.

And in Munich, I learned that studying a certain Cranach Venus through the eyes of D'Abernon had sharpened my pleasure in it. 'Let me take you on a tour,' he said one day. 'I'll show you every Cranach painting in existence. We'll begin in Paris and afterward move on to Vienna, Budapest, and Berlin. Then I'll take you back home and *you* can show *me* the Cranachs in the Metropolitan Museum.'

I asked, 'When could we do it?' And, for the first time called him Edgar.

'Whenever you like.'

I suggested a time when I knew Mr E. would be tied to New York with his chores for the Actors' Equity.

'Next spring,' I suggested.

'That will be just right.'

I was beginning to find a greater warmth and sympathy with D'Abernon than I had ever known. For years I'd been aware that my opinions irritated Mr E., so I tried to smother them. But now, to find that a man whose intelligence awed me was interested in what I thought began to give me self-confidence.

I admired D'Abernon's courage to make such statements as, 'One can be too kind to widows and orphans'; his viewpoint that charity is quite often exhibitionism, a form of social climbing or a snide feeling of guilt, delighted me.

Mr E. contended that socialism would produce a better or even a different type of ruling class. D'Abernon thought otherwise and laughed at such pretensions. He was tough, no doubt about it, but he was not a hypocrite.

There was a case in point that involved Mr E.'s Rolls-Royce sports car. He had whirled us into Vienna one day and the next morning at breakfast was extolling Vienna as one of the first cities in Europe to install a socialist government. Mr E.'s encomium to Vienna was presently interrupted by a tap on the door. Answering it, he was encountered by two officials in uniform who presented him with a demand of an enormous tax bill for bringing his luxury sports car into the city.

Mr E.'s monumental outrage over Viennese larceny made me leave the room in order not to burst out laughing in his face.

It was nearing time when my high-brow rendezvous with Edgar D'Abernon was to start. I was to sail for France; to be met by Edgar at Le Havre and enter into our cerebral love affair, in which the Elder Cranach would play Cupid.

Then, idly glancing through *The New York Times* one morning, I happened on a headline that caused my entire future to collapse: 'Sudden death of Viscount D'Abernon in London.' Our touch-me-not love affair of such long duration was never to reach a climax.

Maybe there'd have been no complete satisfaction in that cerebral affair, but it had caused me to fall out of love with Mr E.

For six years we traveled about Europe in search of throat specialists; or visited out-of-the-way cure places, with which

Mr E. was soon bored and, declaring them no good, we continued our search. It was an aimless life but I enjoyed it; being responsible for Mr E.'s well-being had become a habit that still provided me with a satisfactory *raison d'être*, while Mr E. was more than content to nurse his fascinating ailment. At any rate, the sterile adulation with which I'd once looked on Mr E. was replaced by an appraisal of him that was downright amusing.

An actor at heart, he could substitute pantomime for dialogue, extemporizing little scenes which frequently made him the life of the party. He had discovered a remarkable attention-getter; one he could carry in his pocket. It was a small square of black cardboard covered with waxed paper, on which he wrote words that were clearly visible. Then, by lifting the waxed paper, the words disappeared as if by magic. Mr E. could attract attention with that little gimmick in any group of people, no matter how eminent.

One afternoon in Rome we were being entertained at the Royal Palace by King Victor Emmanuel and his superior, Il Duce. And on that occasion Mr E., aided by his little gadget, outshone all the other guests in the room. He so impressed the King that His Majesty scarcely left Mr E.'s side (which might be a clue as to why Mussolini had been able to annex the regime). Nobody paid any attention to me, and I was free to take everything in, which was the way I liked it.

But as time went on, Mr E. would sometimes get careless, forget to whisper and talk out loud. This lapse became particularly noticeable in Paris, where he was trying to impress a certain pretty socialite who was hard of hearing. Ruth Kresge was so fascinating that she had converted deafness into charisma. So when Mr E. couldn't manage to be heard across a crowd of Ruthie's admirers, he spoke in tones of bell-like clarity.

Be it to the credit of his disarming naïveté, charm, and an egomania that was utterly childlike, nobody ever let Mr E. know that we were wise to his shenanigans.

Finally, at long last, came a day when Mr E. was cured. The specialist concerned was Professor Emil Glas of Vienna, who had attained eminence through being on a team of specialists that treated Der Führer when his throat was torn by long sessions of scathing oratory. Now the Viennese school of medicine is more scientific than ours, because it takes into consideration the element of fantasy. One day Professor Glas called for me in private, just as Dr Jackson had done in Philadelphia, but his plan was to perform an 'operation.' During the process the Professor intended to scratch Mr E.'s throat so severely that it would be quite painful for a few days. Following the 'operation,' Mr E. would be presented with a vial of alcohol in which some flecks of white membrane were floating. The Professor would explain them as 'nodes' which he'd removed from Mr E.'s vocal cords and, as soon as his throat healed, he would be able to speak again.

Professor Glas told me, however, that his plan had an element of chance. If Mr E. still preferred to be a fascinating invalid, the 'operation' would be a failure. But if he was fed up with whispering and wanted to return to a normal life, the removal of these 'nodes' would provide a logical reason for his cure. Would I, as next of kin, agree to the experiment? I hated for Mr E. to suffer a sore throat for those few days but the trick seemed worth a risk.

Mr E. was cured! And it was due to a new conversation piece that he could carry in his pocket; the bottle of alcohol with those white specks floating in it. Moreover, he saw to it that his cure was written up in the *New York Times* and letters began to arrive from victims of every kind of throat trouble who wanted the address of Professor Glas in Vienna. The Professor was acclaimed internationally, married a beautiful Viennese blonde, transferred his practice to New York, and a new life opened up for everybody concerned.

In 1927 Mr E. and I settled down to a life of luxury in New York, where my daily companions were H. L. Mencken, the drama critic George Jean Nathan, novelist Joseph Hergesheimer, and Ernest Boyd. But those intellectuals failed to interest Mr E. and, with time on his hands, he took up a new hobby : social climbing. This hobby's greatest advantage was that I would never be a rival; when in society I am so overtaken by a yearning to escape that my eyes cross and I become otherwise unbearable. Mr E., to the contrary, sparkled. With his good looks unflagging interest in the fair sex, and endurance of platitudes, he had every qualification for social success.

Now during the mid-1920s a new spot had come into focus as the 'snob' place to spend the winter : Palm Beach. So it was thence Mr E. turned his fancy. I was naturally loathe to exchange my New York friends for the sort of dolts who frequent pleasure resorts, so I preferred to remain in New York. But Mr E. was heading into strange territory, and he needed a new gimmick to replace the vial-full of alcohol with its little white specks. And what better gimmick than a current best-selling authoress?

As was sometimes the case, Mr E. was disarmingly truthful about the situation. 'I know you hate to leave New York, but the Palm Beach contingent will all want to meet my Buggie and, once I feel at home there, you can go right back to New York.'

Any interest I might have had in a warm climate had been canceled by those early years in Hollywood. There the hot, dry air stings your eyeballs, prickles your skin, causes wrinkles in teen-agers, and brings on aberrations that produce sex crimes of unspeakable obscenity.

In short, I nurtured every objection I could think of to keep from meeting a man who greeted the most awful hazards of life, death, love, and sex with a simply magnificent bravado.

10

Sex with Bravado

AUTHORS who were close to Wilson Mizner have tried to write about him; Dorothy Parker and Gene Fowler both gave up in despair. After Wilson's death, Gene said to me, 'That man was so much larger than life that there's no scale by which to measure him. Most of Wilson's dialogue, if put down on paper, seems either vulgar or obscene.'

One time I came to realize that the greatest of all authors had actually captured the Miznerian brand of bare-faced rascality. It was an occasion when the Pasadena Playhouse was staging the series of Shakespeare's historical plays that include the character of Falstaff. Suddenly, it struck me that the wit of that rapscallion sounded just like Wilson Mizner. But whereas Falstaff was fat, bumbling, and noisy, Wilson was slim, beautiful, and his voice was sexy on the ear.

It was Wilson's quiet manner of speaking, his courtly bearing, his method of voicing ribaldries in very cultured terms that gave him a bizarre sort of elegance. Unlike most wits, he was as good a listener as he was a talker – how else could he have picked up a knowledge of human folly that turned his ignoble operations into demonstrations of applied psychology?

The several books that have been published about Wilson were written by men, which means that they failed to take into account the response he invariably got from women. During the brief period that was covered in the movie, *San Francisco*, which Robert Hopkins and I wrote about Wilson, he had hung out in a glittering palace of sin on the Barbary Coast, among gamblers, honky-tonk musicians (who at that period were inventing ragtime), and 'parlor girls' who were famous the world over for beauty and the fresh enthusiasm they were putting into a stale old profession. There Wilson quite easily came to be a king. His sophistication at the age of twenty amounted to genius and he dressed with a conservative elegance that made him stand out as a gentleman in the crass vulgarity of the Western tenderloin.

At that time Wilson inspired a bit of corn by some would-be Robert Service:

> Wilson Mizner, Frisco's boy
> Born at the Golden Gate,
> Called 'home' the joints where they open wine
> And the suckers pay the freight
> Backed it three ways off the board
> Gambled, loved and sang
> From Hayman's down to the Tip Saloon
> From the click of the dice to the big wheel's tune
> And the foggy dawn comes all too soon
> To the hustlers in the gang.
>
> The parlor girls they laugh and shine
> And despise the guys who open wine
> But their faithless faithful hearts enshrine
> That boy who beezed around.
>
> Too often you'd hear the tearful plaint
> Of a frivolous blonde with a heart that ain't
> 'No, maybe I'm not a gilded saint
> But I love him with all my heart.'

Wilson's height always made him stand a head above the crowd. From earliest youth he was a favorite subject for the lurid press; anecdotes about him were common word of mouth; anyone could know that acquaintanceship with him was fraught with disaster. That he never ran short of victims was due to a courtesy that was as warm as an embrace, and wasn't completely false. For, to Wilson's mind the entire human race was trapped together in a world full of woe and he felt a compassion for mankind that even extended to his victims.

Wilson held a theory that the 'genus sucker' is a masochist who enjoys a true catharsis in being trimmed. And to do the job politely conferred a benefit on a group which usually suffers from neglect. He was extremely considerate of the unpopular. Although credited with the saying: 'Always treat a lady like a whore and a whore like a lady,' the aphorism had no validity for Wilson. He treated the most besotted females and the most dignified matrons with the same gallant respect.

In 1928 Mr E. and I were no sooner established in a suite at the Royal Poinciana than we were summoned to the court of the king of Palm Beach Society, Addison Mizner. Although Addison's operations were legal, he was worthy of kinship with his brother Wilson. He had made a fortune as an architect by providing the rich with fake Spanish *haciendas*. He erected the most elaborate palazzi without any schooling in architecture. (On one job, Addison omitted a staircase and was forced to pretend it was intentional: a flight of steps running up the outside was more artistic.) As a side line Addison operated a factory in West Palm Beach where he manufactured 'antiques.'

Addison, who was called 'Addie' by all the right people, also invented an artificial moon for nights when nature failed to oblige; in one instance he provided a social climber with two moons, a Miznerian improvement on God himself. But one of Addie's most unique innovations was a beverage produced by squeezing the juice from tomatoes and serving it as a cocktail. Had he only turned his factory over to processing tomato juice, he might have been even richer but, a true brother to Wilson, he preferred to gyp the public with fake antiques.

Addie, in his early fifties, was tall, and fat to boot. The spacious apartment from which he held forth was furnished with genuine antiques; one of which was the self-portrait of a Mizner ancestor, Sir Joshua Reynolds, which added to the over-all air of prestige.

Addie was accustomed to loll in an overstuffed chair that was almost as big as a bed. From this vantage point he functioned not only as monarch but as his own court jester, his cracks having that element so acceptable to high society, of being tinged with a rather female bitchiness. That the two brothers adored each other was always camouflaged by their attitude of mutual contempt. 'The son-of-a-bitch would shoot me,' said Addison, 'just to make book on which way I'd fall!'

Every afternoon at five, the chosen among us used to gather around Addie's big chair for an hour's gossip before time to dress for the evening; Addie adored the beautiful and the light-of-heart. Among his favorites was the lovely New York debutante Marjorie Oelrichs, who later scampered out of the Social Register to marry Eddie Duchin. (Today their son Peter holds the same place as Court Musician to New York society as did his father.) Marge was always trailed by her mother, known as Big Marge. Soft, plump, and beautiful, she was a high-society version of Mae West. Her voice was a sort of sexy wheeze but, contrary to Mae, her brain was like a bag of popcorn.

In due time other members of Addie's court came to include Dick Barthelmess and his very social wife Jessica. She was an heiress and Dick was wealthy from his long career as a film star. He was one of the very few movie personalities content to retire while still young. The numerous Warburton clan from Philadelphia frequented Addie's *salon*. (I've never known a Philadelphian who wasn't a downright 'character'; possibly a defence mechanism resulting from the dullness of their native habitat.) And a spectacular pal of Addie's was Evalyn McLean, the owner of the unlucky Hope Diamond. She was gay, giddy, not to say slap-happy, and was trailed at all times by security agents; men of bulk who took a dim view of the world's most famous gem. The Hope Diamond looked like a piece of pale green glass cut from a beer bottle; its beauty was as nonexistent as the Emperor's new clothes.

Addie was forever being gifted with knickknacks by Evalyn and one day she showed up followed by her chauffeur, who was carrying a radio. The butler installed it near Addie's big chair but when it was switched on, its response was a series of meaningless squawks. Ultimately a repairman discovered that the works had been jammed by the Hope Diamond, which Evalyn had thoughtlessly dropped into its bowels for safekeeping.

Another slaphappy member of Addie's court was his nephew Horace, a dilettante airplane pilot. Horace would take a plane into the air without even checking on whether it had landing gear.

The ruling princess of Addie's Court, and a Mizner to the core, was his niece Ysobel. No young woman was ever so lacking in vanity. Had she made any attempt, Ysobel could have been pretty. She just wasn't interested. She furthermore gave the lie to a time-honored fairy tale; she could have taken the Prince away from any dressed-up Cinderella. One was charmed and tantalized by everything Ysobel said or did.

One day a tiresome stranger inflicted herself on our group, claiming some sort of distant connection with the Mizner family. The lady kept addressing Ysobel as 'Cousin Ysobel' until the latter politely remarked, 'Pray cease calling me your cousin, Madam; you see, I'm illegitimate.'

The Mizner nihilism may seem to have been caused by lack of feeling but, like the Asquiths in London, they constituted a unique and outlandish minority which had produced a sort of chauvinistic adoration for each other. When tragedy struck the Mizners, their reaction was to face it with ribaldry and cheat Fate out of making dupes of them.

It was inevitable that Horace would crack up in his plane and when he did, Wilson advised me of the tragedy in a letter: 'Horace's demise resembled throwing an egg into an electric fan and proved a great joke on his hordes of creditors.' And here follows a rare touch of Miznerian sentiment: 'I don't suppose Horace minded it much – and surely not for long and, inasmuch as sudden death was always loitering at his keester, maybe this was as good a way of going as any.'

I happened to be with Addie on another tragic occasion when a telegram announced the death in San Francisco of his eldest brother, Lansing. The loss was great, for added to their affection for Lansing was family pride in his Miznerian behavior.

Lansing had once been appointed to head a delegation that was sent to New York after the great San Francisco fire to appeal for funds to rebuild the city. A banquet was given by the New York banking fraternity at which such distinguished financiers as Otto Kahn and Jules Bache delivered speeches glorifying the profession which kept the world solvent. Finally, the Chairman asked Lansing to give his views on the attributes that made for a great banker. Lansing rose and made the shortest banquet speech ever uttered. It consisted of one word: 'Circumcision.' The New York bankers lent San Francisco all the money it required and did it in a gale of laughter.

On the day that the telegram brought word of Lansing's death, Addie and I went upstairs to break the tragic news to Wilson. We found him standing at the bureau adjusting his tie. Tossing down the telegram Addie remarked, 'Here's a wire from Frisco that says Lansing just cooled.' 'I wish you'd told me before I put on this red necktie,' said Wilson.

Wilson inhabited a suite under his brother's own roof, but I'd been a regular member of Addie's group for several weeks without ever meeting him. I was told that his nights were spent at the gambling casino run by his friend, Major Bradley, and he slept most of the day.

Addie told me he had tried to force Wilson into the social life of Palm Beach, thinking it would be an anodyne for his disgraceful past.

'I should have known better,' Addie sighed with a mixture of humiliation and pride. 'But I finally inveigled him into going to one of Mrs Stotesbury's formal dinners.'

Now Mrs Stotesbury was a dowager whose parties were as pompous as they were dull and Wilson's entrance into her drawing room that night had been auspicious; his elegant attire and courtly manners made all the other gentlemen dim into insignificance.

Vastly impressed, Mrs Stotesbury launched a conversation with Wilson in which she derided the bad taste of the day, remarking that one hardly knew what to expect next. 'How right you are, dear lady!' Wilson agreed. 'Why, I never set foot outside my own home, without the illusion that I'm up to my ass in vulgarity.'

The horrified gasp that went up from Mrs Stotesbury secured Wilson's release, once and for all, from the social ties with which Addie hoped to bind him.

One afternoon Addie interrupted the chitchat of the tea hour to say, 'Look, Nita, you've spent enough time here on the right side of the tracks. I'm going to escort you over to the wrong side. Come on upstairs.'

Addie led me up a vaulted stone staircase, carpeted in red, and we entered the remote tower inhabited by his brother. No hotel room could have looked less lived-in. It was sparsely furnished, except for one of Addie's fake Spanish beds, where Wilson was reclining in white silk pajamas under a canopy of red brocade. He was engaged in opening a parcel wrapped in newspaper of which there were several others on the counterpane; two had already been opened and they revealed bales of greenbacks held by rubber bands. Although I never found out for sure, I figured they must have been Wilson's percentage as shill for the previous night's take at Major Bradley's.

Wilson was a badly preserved giant of fifty-one. His massive shoulders had begun to sag; his brown hair was flecked with gray, and Time, that silent old bugler, had started to sound the retreat on his hairline. But his head was leonine and looked as rugged as if it were hacked from granite. His expressions were enlivened by a sort of super-human awareness, and he had that arresting feature which the French call *les yeux rapides*. Just the same, his physical fitness was nil; he had given up pastimes that required any motion and settled into the life of a spectator, mesmerized by the travesty of human behavior.

When Addie introduced us, Wilson addressed me most deferentially as 'little lady' and said that Addie had given him a copy of my book which he had not yet had time to read. At which point the butler entered with his breakfast, consisting of a beaker of orange juice to be mixed with a split of champagne; so we left. The famous wit hadn't said anything the least unconventional; the occasion didn't call for it; a wisecrack would only have been showing off. But, Wilson's air of calm authority was eloquent even in silence.

To my youthful eyes, everything about that aging reprobate was exciting: the aura of his reckless past; the challenge of his being a highly unsuitable companion: his air of tranquil assurance, which, as a rule, exists only in men of genius. I fancy the youthful widows of Pablo Picasso, Edward Steichen, and Pablo Casals knew all about that type of sex appeal. Not that it is found only in men of genius; sometimes aging gangsters have the same allure; so do certain Greek tycoons and a few popular entertainers like Frank Sinatra.

After that first meeting, I believe I lay awake all night, wondering if I would ever meet Wilson Mizner again. The question brought forth a reply which was so prompt it took my breath away. The very next afternoon, at teatime, Wilson stalked into his brother's living room. His appearance among that crew of lightweight gossips was unheard of. 'What brought *you* here?' Addie asked. Stating that he had come to make an apology, Wilson gestured toward me. 'I've passed up this little girl's book because I thought it was just a collection of gags. But I read it last night and found it's a lot more than that.'

Whereupon Wilson moved a chair next to mine and remained there until the tea party was over.

II

The Wrong Side of the Tracks Is Livelier

WHILE Mr E. was dining and dancing in luxury with the elite, Wilson took me into a small, cozy refuge he had established. It was a shoddy café and swimming pool on the ocean front. The entire complex was known as Guss'es Baths.

There was a minimum of drinking at Guss'es and the food was elemental; but the company was enchanting. The rarest of all things in American life is charm. We spend billions every year manufacturing fake charm that goes under the heading of 'public relations.' Without it, America would be grim indeed. However, the *real* thing was as native to Wilson's group as the salubrious salt air we breathed.

During the several winters we spent in Palm Beach I was not the only youthful nonconformist to spend the sweet hours of the night sitting around that big table at Guss'es with Wilson; Marge Oelrichs, with whom I had formed a fond attachment, often escaped the chaperonage of her Ma and joined us. Another girlish socialite was Irving Berlin's bride. They had been married in 1926 and Irving would frequently bring Ellin from their honeymoon villa to give her a glimpse of the bewildering manner in which the other half lived.

Addie never showed up at Guss'es; his self esteem wouldn't allow it. But there were others of his set who never missed a session, among them the young, beautiful, rich, and chic Herbert Westons. Minnie Weston could add to the gaiety of any occasion. (Meeting her near Carnegie Hall one day I asked, 'Would you like to take in a concert?' 'A *concert*? Why, I'd rather take in washing!')

After their marriage in 1928 Dick and Jessica Barthelmess were often with us as well as Mary Brown Warburton from the Main Line of Philadelphia, and Wilson's long-time crony E. Ray Goetz.

In his youth, E. Ray had invaded Broadway from up-state Buffalo, to become a lyric writer in collaboration with a much less colorful denizen of Tin Pan Alley named Edgar Leslie. Their songs had just the right touch of homespun naïveté to make a big success. 'The Bells Are Ringing for Me and My Gal' still touches the nation's heart and tickles its ears to the tune of several thousand dollars a year in ASCAP royalties to Ray's estate.

E. Ray was plump and fortyish, with the placid mien of an overfed Buddha. Having long since deserted Tin Pan Alley for a life that brooked less mental strain, E. Ray had spent some time in the Twenties carousing about Europe with Giacomo Puccini when the great composer, beset by lung cancer, was devoting his last months to wine, women, song, *and* cigarettes.

Then there was a short period when E. Ray became an impresario and undertook to bring to the U.S. an incredibly fascinating Spanish singer, Raquel Meller, who was the toast of Paris. She had refused countless offers to appear in New York because of an abysmal fear of crossing the Atlantic. But E. Ray promised to escort her all the way to the U.S. in a Pullman car, whereupon he flashed a lovely, colored picture of the Orient Express he had picked up at Cook's on the Boulevard des Capucines.

E. Ray escorted the beautiful creature onto a boat train, complete with luggage and assorted pets. When forced to embark at Le Havre, he fast-talked Raquel into boarding the

S. S. *Paris*, where she cowered in bed for the entire voyage, fully dressed for the wreck she knew was imminent.

On landing in New York, E. Ray restored her normal mood of cheerful idiocy by promising that, as soon as her engagement was finished, he'd motor her all the way back to Paris in his Dion-Bouton landaulet. Again she believed him, because since the days of Queen Isabella, no Spanish person has ever studied a map. (Possibly Christopher Columbus himself had to bring one with him from Italy.)

Raquel Meller was a staggering success in New York. In her song, 'La Violetera,' she passed down the aisles tossing bunches of violets to bald-headed men who snapped for them like guppies snapping at a swimmer. But when time came for Raquel to return to Paris, she was again forced onto a ship and her faith in E. Ray Goetz was shattered forever.

E. Ray's greatest contribution to the gaiety of nations was as the producer of the early musicals of Cole Porter. E. Ray himself coined the theme that 'Fifty Million Frenchmen Can't Be Wrong.' But he looked on the box office as his own voluminous pocket, a fact that used to cut in heavily on Cole's royalties. I once heard a crashing bore comment about Ray's lack of probity, at which Cole withered him with the remark, 'But *Mr Goetz* is very good company!'

However, not all the contingent at Guss'es Bath's were such outstanding favorites of fortune. One of the transient guests who, to quote Wilson, was 'wanted everywhere and welcome nowhere' was a gentleman of impeccable manners and immense prestige who had just been released from the Federal Penitentiary at Atlanta where he'd been sent by an outraged society matron for whom, at a price, he'd made life worth the living. Wilson financed his pal to a couple of weeks in the sun to get rid of the prison pallor that might hamper a return to his career. Nobody knew his name but he was called the Baron, which fitted nicely.

Another unfortunate was a famous Hollywood film star who was hooked on drugs but lacked the coordination to keep herself in supply. She was a lively companion, with that far-out, crazy type of wit which results when the mind is artificially released from all boundaries. Wilson realized that the hopeless young zany would get no help except from someone like himself who'd known a yen for drugs, and he once drove all night to bring her a fix from Miami. (Cheerful postscript: that star has lived to middle age in Hollywood and, through some very odd behavior in supermarkets, earned enough attention to keep her happily in the public eye.)

I had learned of Wilson's own drug addiction from Addie, who had persuaded him to undergo a cure when Wilson first settled in Palm Beach. In those days drug addiction was mentioned only in whispers, but Wilson made it a subject for his most explosive jokes. And why not? Anybody who lays himself open to the perfectly foreseeable clobbering of a drug habit has got to be a fool. So Wilson made the fact pay off in laughs.

But Wilson's cure had consisted of the instant withdrawal known as 'cold turkey' and was such sheer torture that, for once, it caused the joke of Wilson's addiction to lose its point. Like most giants, he had no resistance to pain but he stuck it through to the end and went on medical record as a unique case, insofar as he could take any drug or abstain.

Another habitué of Guss'es was a gorgeous corn-fed beauty from the Middle West who was shameless in her pursuit of Wilson. One evening she joined us, coming from a cocktail party where she'd gotten tight, and made the proclamation that her only desire in life was to become 'passion's playground' for Wilson Mizner. That a beautiful blonde could destroy her sex appeal by such embarrassing dialogue, when all she needed for success was to keep her mouth shut, delighted me no end. It reminded me of a comment Jack Barrymore once made about his daughter. 'Diana is a horse's arse,' said Jack, 'quite a pretty one, but still a horse's arse.'

Any liaison between Wilson and that blond nincompoop was out of the question but her lack of success never stopped Louisa from tracking him down. Moreover, she was always welcome at Addie's because he sold her mother countless artifacts to embellish a mansion in Duluth.

Louisa would listen to Wilson with the dewy gaze of a Desdemona enraptured by Othello, regardless of the fact that his anecdotes invariably revealed Wilson as a failure. There was one minor venture in which he had joined E. Ray. It began in Berlin, where they had unearthed a German inventor who had perfected a process by which oil paintings could be reproduced so that they could scarcely be told from the originals. Wilson and E. Ray scooped up some of those masterpieces and, on arrival at the New York Customs, skilfully managed to be arrested for smuggling 'art treasures' into the country. This error of the Customs Department resulted in valuable publicity for an art gallery the two planned to open on Fifth Avenue. Their idea was to sell the replicas in wholesale lots to hotels and religious organizations. But Wilson lost their first churchly client when he quoted the price on Leonardo da Vinci's 'Last Supper' as 'five dollars a plate.'

Another venture which failed through Wilson's inclination to put fun ahead of business was a gambling palace he operated in a stately mansion on Long Island. At that time Wilson had an indigent friend whose one single asset was a resemblance to William Howard Taft, then Chief Justice of the United States Supreme Court. Wilson placed his comrade on the payroll; his job was to sit in the parlor and casually leaf through a copy of *The New York Times*. It was Wilson's idea that his pal, being mistaken for the Chief Justice, would give the establishment an aura of respectability which it actually didn't deserve.

But the fake William Howard Taft found his job tedious. In the first place, he had never learned to read; his sole literary occupation was to look at the pictures in the *Police Gazette*. So one evening, fed up with the *Times*, he got tight, made overtures to a bus boy and, on being repulsed, stabbed him with a steak knife.

The wound was a mere scratch and its perpetrator quickly hustled out of sight, but there had been enough witnesses to start a rumor that the Chief Justice of the U.S. Supreme Court was overly fond of little boys. News filtered through to Washington that a Taft look-alike was being used as a shill for a gambling house and a federal indictment closed Wilson's establishment down.

The presence of big Louisa at Guss'es Baths spurred Wilson to outdo himself in ribaldry, as if he took delight in shattering the romantic aura with which her virgin fancy endowed him. One of his scabrous tales concerned an event that took place when he was a youth in San Francisco. A gay and pretty inhabitant of the Barbary Coast asked Wilson to take her on a trip to Honolulu. He even agreed to do a little honest labor in order to finance the holiday. A certain insurance company had offered him a fee if he could lure the wife of California's leading banker into signing up for a policy. It was arranged for Wilson to take tea with the lady and he was then told that her application must be accompanied by that certain specimen necessary for a kidney test; a fact which Wilson with typical Falstaffian bawdiness took in his stride. Sauntering blithely up from the Barbary Coast, he kept the rendezvous. But when his hostess entered the parlor of her Nob Hill mansion that afternoon, she proved to be of such beauty, charm, and high style that

Wilson was beguiled. It was not until the lovely creature had signed the policy that he suddenly remembered that necessary specimen. To have mentioned so embarrassing a matter would have harmed the idyllic entente which had grown up between them. But as usual, a way to evade the impasse crossed Wilson's mind; seeing that his girl friend was to be the main beneficiary of the deal, why not ask *her* to supply the required specimen? Thus was Wilson free to take a chivalrous leave of the beautiful applicant and return in triumph to the Barbary Coast.

But wise guy that Wilson was, he had once more outsmarted himself. The chemist who made an analysis for the application reacted with something akin to horror and turned it down. In telling us of that debacle Wilson, like a cad, put the blame on his girl. 'Why, in her state of physical well-being, she couldn't have financed a trip on the ferry boat to Benicia!'

That incident was not the worst antiaphrodisiac with which Wilson regaled big, blond Louisa. He told of another shattering humiliation that befell him in a Chicago hospital where he had been booked for minor surgery. On the day of the operation a beautiful nurse with whom he'd been whiling away his leisure, wheeled a cot into Wilson's room on which she was to trundle him to the surgery. Wishing to impress the pretty creature with his nonchalance, Wilson put on a chic dressing gown and declared he would cover the distance on foot. But, on entering the operating theater he was suddenly confronted by blinding lights, a surgical team in masks and funeral white coats, and an array of death-dealing cutlery; Wilson fell foul of that reaction of a small boy who is suddenly frightened out of all control. Wilson told us of helplessly standing there while the embarrassing demonstration went on ... and on ... and on. The surgical team pretended to occupy itself with various preparations. The pretty nurse found she was required in another department and withdrew. As a crowning degradation, the floor had to be mopped up and sterilized before the operation began.

But, to the credit of Wilson's amazing insouciance and charm, poor dumb Louisa could listen to that unsavory tale and still see him as a figure of romance. Many smart girls would have done the same and one of them was definitely me.

12

It's Love That Makes the World Go Square

EARLY in the 1930s Wilson paid me a compliment that touched me to the heart; he set me straight about his nefarious career. 'You're just a kid beginning to get around,' he told me, 'I wouldn't want my example to give you a wrong steer.' He quoted a saying that had gone the rounds in his heyday, 'The lobster is the wise guy after all.' ('Lobster' being used then as we use 'square' today.) 'All of us are born with traits like optimism, faith, and loyalty,' Wilson continued. 'Just don't deny them for the hollow pretense of being "smart."'

Wilson went on to admit that a statement he often made of 'work being beneath the dignity of any red-blooded man' was ridiculous. 'The con games I've invented all took more work than any legal effort. And not one of them ever paid off with anything like permanent cash.'

Disarmed by his frank avowal, I asked wide-eyed, 'Why haven't you followed your own advice?' Wilson's features broke into that grin, halfway between amusement and resignation, of the fellow who knows that Fate always holds a slap-stick aloft, ready to smack down every wise guy.

'I've always been like the rabbit that thinks it can block a Mack truck!'

Wilson made that confession just after he had amassed several million dollars as a realtor in Palm Beach. He had invented a new type of salesmanship which consisted in advertising a strictly local commodity in national magazines. That scheme is one of Wilson's gifts to posterity. Advertisements are still published in which oldsters are pictured cavorting in a resurgence of sex on a piece of Florida real estate.) Wilson's mail-order campaign enabled him to sell lots that never emerged from the tide. He used to boast that his merchandise extended clear to the shores of Cuba.

But in 1927, the Florida Boom burst just as Wilson instinctively knew it would, and after going broke he was hauled into court by a purchaser of one of his underwater lots. The judge fixed an accusing eye on Wilson and demanded, 'Didn't you tell this man that he could grow nuts on his land?' 'The gentleman misunderstood, your Honor,' Wilson answered respectfully. 'What I actually said was that he could go nuts on his land.' And as Wilson had so often done in the past, he was forced to jump bail and beat a sheriff across the state line.

However, *Le Bon Dieu* who looks after publicans and sinners had provided Wilson with a gorgeous last frontier: Hollywood.

At the time Wilson arrived there, I was in New York living through the manic era before the crash of 1929. He and I were separated by an entire continent, but we kept in touch. In an effort to establish some sort of kinship, Wilson had taken to calling me 'Mama Nita.' The nickname was a double joke; he was too old by a generation to be my son while my wind-blown bob and knee-high skirts would never have been worn by any mother.

On Mother's Day in 1929 Wilson sent me a telegram which read: 'The great creator in his loving kindness made mothers so that everyone no matter how unworthy might have someone to love him supremely. Affectionate greetings to my mother this Mother's Day. Willie.' (Wilson had either written that telegram with tongue-in-cheek or perhaps he actually was revelling in the sentiment of a square.)

On New Year's Day of 1930 came the message: 'Dear Mama Nita, I've known many years and they were all lousy so take a hint from your loving boy and don't put too much confidence in this one.'

And then in December 1931 I, too, moved to Hollywood and we would be together practically every day until Wilson died.

From his very entrance into Hollywood, Wilson, true to form, dominated the scene. Finding no spot where a man of his inertia could loaf in comfort, he opened a restaurant in partnership with Herb Somborn, a sportsman who had been one of Gloria Swanson's husbands. They called it the Brown Derby, after that emblem of Wilson's political pal, Al Smith. Ultimately the venture grew into a chain of restaurants; Wilson's only enterprise that was to be a legitimate success.

Mr E. had started our marriage off by demanding freedom to choose his own associates; so he had to allow me the same privilege. And because I'd always had men friends, he chose to ignore that my feelings for Wilson might be of quite a different caliber.

That our sentiment was largely of the 'barroom' type made it all the more potent. Night after night Wilson and I might sit in a moody underworld café where he'd order the orchestra to play 'Melancholy Baby' and urge the violinist to 'Make it sad for the little lady!' So, just as in a Humphrey Bogart movie, the scene was much more romantic than any moonlit pastoral.

Sometimes we were in the company of such delectables as W.C. Fields, Jack Barrymore, Tallulah Bankhead, Carole Lombard, Gene Fowler, or Joe Frisco, who was a notable victim of the Santa Anita track. Along with W. C. Fields, Joe was an enemy of the California climate. He would complain that 'Sometimes it's hot and sometimes it's cold; a man never

115

knows what to hock.' One evening when Joe ordered apple
pie the waitress said, 'Sorry, Mr Frisco, there's no more apple
pie.' 'Then fake it!' answered Joe.

Soon after Wilson arrived in the film capital, the head of
production at Warner Brothers' Studio, Darryl Zanuck,
inveigled Wilson into allowing a secretary to trail him on his
aimless wanderings and take down his remarks in shorthand.
They were then turned over to the script department for in-
tegration into filmplays. Some of the wisecracks gotten off
by Humphrey Bogart and Jimmy Cagney in their gangster
comedies originated with Wilson.

A plot that Wilson ad-libbed one night while sitting in
the Derby won the Oscar after his death as the best original
filmplay of 1932. It was titled *One Way Passage* : a story of
two underworld lovers on an ocean voyage who knew that at
the end of their journey the law would separate them for life.

Finally, Wilson's disrespect for health caught up with him
at last. He lay trapped in a cheerless suite at the Ambassador
Hotel, where he had camped out ever since his escape from
Florida. It was in the cards that Wilson should pass on. Hollywood would soon be finished as the nation's last frontier of
glamour and larceny; after which there would be no more
frontiers.

Trying to put up a show of courage, I went to visit Wilson
every afternoon accompanied by Mark Kelly, a sports writer
on the *Los Angeles Times*. Wilson's huge frame would be
sprawled on a twin bed and his face half-covered by an ap-
pliance through which his breath came in painful spasms.
Explaining that oxygen mask, Wilson said, 'Without this,
I'd be gasping like a grounded mullet.'

One day Mark, an ardent Catholic, brought along a crucifix to hang over Wilson's bed. 'Do you think that's going to
do me any good?' Wilson asked dubiously. 'I know it will.

pal!' Mark declared. Wilson cocked an eye at the crucifix. 'But just look at the predicament the poor guy got into *himself*,' he argued.

Every day Wilson's breathing became more labored. And every day he grew more heartbreakingly cheerful. Finally, a moment came when I could no longer keep back my tears. 'What's the matter, Mama Nita?' he asked. 'Can't you take it?' Unable to control my feelings, I started for the door. 'Wait a moment, Mama! Don't run out on your boy like this! It won't be long now before the Main Event.'

It wasn't long, indeed. Before Mark and I could visit Wilson again, the Main Event took place.

At the studio the next day, wandering through the Alley in a state of shock, I ran into Walter Wanger. A movie producer, Walter was one of the few gentlemen of culture in that outlaw profession. He adored Wilson and stopped me to say, 'Well, honey, from now on the Hereafter is going to be a much better place!'

As a matter of fact, even this side of the Hereafter is better, for me, because of Wilson Mizner. Some of my dearest friends are close because they were friends of his. Paulette Goddard, when a bride for the first time, had married Wilson's young partner when the two used to ply a glamorous trade as international gamblers on ocean liners. Ruth Dubonnet and I still call each other by nicknames Wilson gave us. I am 'Mug' and she is 'Pal.' And Ray Goetz, who tried to follow Wilson in everything he ever did, asked me to marry him.

The date of Ray's proposal reads : *June 16th, 1934 – dinner with Ray in Hollywood at Sign of the Cock.*

With no preamble at all, Ray started out, 'Look, Baby, will you divorce Emerson and marry me?'

The proposal coming from that seasoned playboy in his mid-forties, was a shocker. It was true Ray had gone through a scrambled, show-biz marriage with the French musical-comedy star, Irene Bordoni. And a gossip column had once connected us romantically : 'Ray Goetz is making the scene of West 52nd Street speakeasies with a pint-sized look-alike of his ex-wife.' But for Ray to marry again was as unthinkable as if Bluebeard were to give himself a shave.

'When did *this* idea hit you?' I asked.

'That day Wilson said he wanted you for keeps. Then I suddenly wanted you, too.'

It would be hard to conjure up a free soul like Wilson Mizner ever making a statement which puts a man forever in a trap. So the explanation involves a series of complicated events which began at Palm Beach in 1927.

A group consisting of Irving and Ellin Berlin, Marge Oelrichs, Dick Barthelmess, and I were holding forth at Addie's during the gossip hour when Ray Goetz wandered in to report a scoop. He had been about to enter Wilson's bedroom when he was suddenly stopped by a glimpse through the open door of Wilson and big, stupid Louisa from Duluth. Wilson, in his dressing gown, was pouring champagne and his intentions toward the gorgeous blonde were unmistakable. Ray had withdrawn without being seen and he hurried downstairs to spread the gossip.

As I listened to Ray's account of that assignation, a sense of betrayal shot through me that was as acute as it was unwarranted. Wilson and I had been inseparable from the day we met, but we never talked about anything serious and he had never said a single word to indicate he 'cared.'

As I sat there, outraged over being a 'castoff,' Addie began to voice an alarm. It so happened that Louisa's mother was buying huge quantities of the antiques Addie manufactured. And her daughter, as a carefully nurtured virgin, was counted on to marry a title and spearhead the family out of Duluth. But a liaison with Addie's disgraceful brother could instantly wreck the ambitions of her Ma and alienate her from Addie himself.

Speaking up in alarm, he said, 'Quick, Nita! Get to the phone and break up that tryst before Wilson loses me my best customer!'

Suddenly I recognized Addie's plea as a challenge to find out whether I had the power to wrest Wilson away from that sex-bitten debutante. Her virginity was in the balance, there was little time to think but I went to the phone and, with the others straining their ears to hear, I began to test my prowess.

'I've got to see you right away!' I told Wilson.

'I'm busy going over some accounts,' he lied cheerfully. 'I'll meet you in an hour.'

I watched Addie's face register alarm; another hour and Louisa would be a fallen woman. 'It's got to be *right now!*' I insisted.

'What's the matter, Mama Nita; is something wrong?'

It required a quick moment to think up an answer to that one. But, taking a long chance on Wilson's credulity, I gasped, 'John Emerson has found out about us!'

I waited in suspense because there was nothing for John Emerson to find out. After a short pause Wilson asked, 'Where are you now?' I lied and told him I was home and then, without a moment's hesitation, he said 'I'll be right over!'

I hung up and announced in triumph 'Louisa is now being left flat!'

Relieved as Addie was, he began to have suspicions. 'Look, Nita, *is* there something between you two brigands that *could* upset John?'

'Not a thing!'

Addie shook his head in shame. 'The idiot's so accustomed to being guilty he never questions a verdict.'

At this point Ray suggested we *all* go over to my place, encounter Wilson on his arrival, and let him know he'd been had. At first Addie hesitated to participate in that joke on his brother, but he finally agreed.

We trooped over to my place and, en route, Dick Barthelmess expanded the joke. I would meet Wilson alone, while the others went into hiding to spy on the scene. And no sooner did Wilson barge into the house than I gasped out that Mr E. was on his way to confront him. Now, the only logical rejoinder would have been 'Confront me with *what?*'

But what Wilson actually said was: 'If Emerson knows about us, we're free to go away together for keeps!'

Electrified by his proposal, I was speechless. But then Addie, intent on keeping his brother from further humiliation, stepped out of hiding. 'I'm sorry we did this to you, Willie, but I asked Nita to get you away from that big blonde before you wrecked my business deals with her Ma.'

As Wilson stood there dazed and unable to utter a word, Addie let him have another barb. 'What did you *think* John Emerson could find out about you two?'

Wilson rallied to the insult on his credulity. 'Husbands have second sight; I was convinced he'd read my mind!'

Wilson's confession that he 'cared' shook me to the very heart. I'd have given half my future life to erase the trick I'd just played on him.

But fate hadn't yet finished with Wilson's humiliation. The other witnesses to it emerged from hiding and Wilson, the smartest guy in any town, learned the full extent to which he'd been done in.

Turning on me with that sheepish grin I knew so well, he announced, 'I wish you were dead!'

I had tossed a monkey wrench into the love of my lifetime for the hollow pretense of being smart, *just as Wilson himself had warned me never to do.*

Even so, Wilson seemed to forget he'd wished I were dead and our activities went on innocently as before. However, deep down underneath, my jealousy of that blonde still rankled. How could Wilson ever have planned her defilement, if I were the one he wanted 'for keeps'?

But then, one evening when we were all holding forth at Guss'es Baths, some newcomer asked what had become of Louisa. Wilson spoke up jauntily, like the cad he was : 'The last time I saw the big broad was one afternoon when I was trying to get rid of a terrific yen for the wife of a friend.'

Wilson veered off onto some other subject, but he had given me a brand new fact to ponder : that I *myself* had been the heroine of his tryst with a blond sex-pot. Like most females, I had stupidly failed to realize that a casual affair need have no bearing at all on romance, love, or even fidelity. But now that I'd learned that lesson, it was apparently too late.

13

Life in a Glamour Factory

SHOW business is the best possible therapy for remorse. I've known deserted brides to take fresh interest in life by sweeping up the stage in some godforsaken regional theater. At the time when the New York banker Walter Rosen died, after years of a marriage that had been an uninterrupted love affair, we all said 'Lucie Rosen won't survive the loss of Walter very long!' But friends of Lucie pressed her into turning their great estate in Westchester into a music center. And Lucie, as doyenne of the annual Caramoor Music Festival, was very soon the merriest of widows. To update Shakespeare, Hamlet needn't have warned Ophelia to 'Get thee to a nunnery.' Today he could better have said, 'Get thee to a Hollywood film factory.' At any rate, MGM turned my cramped emotional life into a festival.

Mr E. and I occupied a house on Elm Drive in the heart of Beverly Hills, an area which resembles any prosperous Midwestern suburb. Its architecture is slick and its gardens well manicured.

Our house looked quite cozy and across the street there was a charming cottage of Cotswold design where Humphrey Bogart lived with his not-so-famous actress wife, Mayo Methot. But life on our block would never be dull. In the early 1940s Lauren Bacall would be on the horizon as a zooming star and the next Mrs Humphrey Bogart. In fact all Beverly Hills was a mishmash of marital unrest, frustrated ambition, and professional jealousy, all of which I could easily escape because the studio became my home.

A typical day for me was to begin writing in my own room. At 4 a.m., I was delightfully alone with a sneaky feeling of freedom from having to protect Mr E.'s ego throughout all his waking hours. I was lucky because he slept late.

After five hours of work, I was at the studio by ten and still free because Mr E. didn't show up until after lunch. Better still, he loved to sit for hours in his suite of offices in the executive building meticulously crossing t's, dotting i's, and putting commas into my work before he submitted it to Irving. But ours, in many ways, was better than most Hollywood marriages. Moreover, what domesticity, however ideal, could compete with the excitement of a movie studio?

All MGM was divided into two parts. Its main section was given over to executive offices, projection rooms, enormous sound stages, wardrobe and make-up departments, dressing rooms, and the mysterious laboratories for the processing of film.

A broad avenue ran through the main lot. It was known as the Alley and through it flowed the lifeblood of the studio. There was a constant parade of actors on their way to sound stages; Irving en route to projection rooms accompanied by a group of aides; other producers, aping the boss, followed by galleries of 'yes-men,' of which Irving had none.

On the enormous back lot there were outdoor sets, some of them permanent. There was a village square with homes, shops, and a church, where the Andy Hardy series was filmed in the late 1930s. There was a block of brownstone fronts for New York exteriors. There were city slums and tropical jungles with rivers, ponds, and a waterfall. There was an enormous tank with inch-thick glass walls. It was eventually large enough to float the H.M.S. *Bounty* of *Mutiny* fame, and so deep that years later Esther Williams or a rubber whale could be photographed underwater.

My office was in an old cottage; a relic of the time when Culver City was a low-income residential district. I shared it with Lionel Barrymore, who suffered from arthritis and couldn't negotiate a long flight of stairs leading to the dressing rooms. Next door was a cottage which housed the school for contract kids. It was there that little Mickey Rooney and Judy Garland would get their education. They used to dash in and out at odd hours making a lot of noise, about which Lionel would gripe with monumental indignation.

Lionel was gifted in many different ways : a symphony he composed was introduced by the Minneapolis Symphony Orchestra; he turned out some very professional dry-point etchings. And Lionel was the only actor I ever knew who, when he forgot his lines, would extemporize others that were totally in character. It used to amuse me to hear some second-rate scrivener fume about Lionel changing his script, because Lionel generally improved on it.

There were long stretches when Lionel, not acting, and I, awaiting a call from Irving, wrote a play together. It was titled *Old Buddha* and concerned the Dowager Empress of China, showing that fierce old despot at the mercy of a piddling Yankee dentist she'd been forced to import to make her a set of false teeth.

We intended the play for Lionel's sister, Ethel, but when she read it she couldn't stomach the casual attitude toward gore that the role required. Ethel tossed *Old Buddha* into a trash can and, there being no other star who could give our Empress the right combination of majesty and seething humiliation, we lost interest. (I've just read the play again and find it hilarious, which I can say without boasting because ninety per cent of it is Lionel's.)

When the writers were all moved into the new Thalberg

Building, a directory in the downstairs lobby listed, at one time or another, every important American, English, French, and Hungarian author in the world : Zoe Akins, Maxwell Anderson, Michael Arlen, Vicki Baum, Robert Benchley, Stephen Vincent Benét, Scott Fitzgerald, Robert Flaherty, Moss Hart, Ben Hecht, Samuel Hoffenstein, Sidney Howard, Aldous Huxley, Christopher Isherwood, George S. Kaufman, George Kelly, Frederick Lonsdale, Charles MacArthur, Ferenc Molnar, Dorothy Parker, S. J. Perelman, Ernest Vajda, and John Van Druten.

Those authors were signed on short-term contracts which in most cases were never renewed; for there is a knack about dramatic writing which some very legitimate talents can't master. The scripts Scott Fitzgerald wrote just wouldn't play. It thus came about that the studio's product was actually supplied by only about ten per cent of its writing staff. The most reliable were women : Frances Marion, Bess Meredith, Sonja Levine, Vicki Baum, and Jane Murfin. The three latter had sound literary backgrounds; on the other hand, Frances Marion originated some of the best of the MGM films by talking her plots out in conference, after which the scripts were written by other authors.

Irving didn't have a great deal of respect for us scribblers. We irritated him as a sort of necessary evil. 'Damn it,' he told me one day, 'I can keep tabs on everybody else in the studio and see whether or not they're doing their jobs. But I can never tell what's going on in those so-called brains of yours.'

While I'd met some of those literary big shots elsewhere, there were many I'd have liked to know but had to neglect through sheer surfeit of riches. It was pleasant running into them in the Alley but there was never time enough to make new friends. What leisure I *did* have was spent with Zoe Akins, Charlie MacArthur, Ben Hecht, and Aldous

Huxley, with all of whom I'd been on fond terms in New York.

I tried to avoid Scott Fitzgerald, although I'd known him and Zelda intimately in New York, Paris, and on the Riviera. I liked them well enough when they were sober which, alas, was all too seldom. When drunk, their behavior could be downright hazardous or, at best, pretty tiresome. Zelda had a habit of stripping in public which might be described today as 'chutzpah,' of which the rule is, 'If you've got it, flaunt it.' But to flaunt something you haven't got can be a mistake. Zelda's face could have landed her in the front line of the Ziegfeld Follies, but she should have kept her bosom strictly under wraps.

Zelda's strip tease could be compared with Tallulah's, whose figure suffered the identical drawback. But Tallulah flaunted her nudity through an impish desire to shock, whereas Zelda felt that hers was delectable.

Another disturbing memory of Scott and Zelda concerns a night in Paris when Mr E. and I were on our way to a party at Gertrude Stein's and dropped by their hotel to take them with us. When we arrived, Scott and Zelda were tight and the baby was in its crib bawling her poor little head off. Zelda was afraid Scotty's screams might get them evicted, so she filled a nursing bottle with warm water, sugar, and gin and then, looking as lovely as a Botticelli Madonna, she fed the mixture to Scotty. As we went into the night, the baby was already in a stupor, untroubled over being left alone and drunk in strange surroundings.

During a time when we were all staying at the Hotel du Cap in Antibes, Zelda had just had her appendix removed. She'd been released from hospital on condition that she remain sober and keep to her bed until the surgeon removed her stitches. Late one night, Scott stumbled into their room and found that Zelda had disappeared, leaving an empty gin bottle at her bedside. He went looking for her and, on reaching the veranda, finally spotted Zelda through the darkness. She'd gone for a swim and her head was barely visible, bobbing far out in the icy, rough Mediterranean.

Scott dashed through the lobby calling for help and waking everybody up. Finally a lifeguard was alerted and sent off to the rescue. We all gathered on the veranda, too intent on Zelda's fate to notice that Scott was busily dashing the porch furniture down into the sea; perhaps as something to which Zelda might cling, but possibly just for the fun of breaking up furniture.

When the lifeguard pulled Zelda ashore limp, pale, and shivering, she'd sobered up enough to explain her escapade. 'I had a fever of a hundred and four and thought a swim might cool me off.' That the stitches in Zelda's wound held fast and that she didn't drown or get pneumonia could only have been due to the special providence that looks after fools and alcoholics.

But my most horrendous experience with the Fitzgeralds took place one night in Great Neck. Scott had picked me up in New York to take me to their place for dinner. I didn't notice he'd been drinking, but we'd only gone a little way when I realized my error. By a miracle, we arrived at their country house without an accident, and, once there, I found to my relief that Zelda was cold sober.

Scott soon disappeared and then a very informal butler shuffled in and announced dinner. Zelda and I took our places at table. Presently Scott came in, silent and glowering, and proceeded to turn the latch on the dining-room door. Then, facing Zelda and me he announced : 'Now I'm going to kill you two!'

We hadn't time to get up from table before Scott started pitching things at us from very close range : heavy things; two enormous candelabras with lighted candles, a water carafe, a metal wine cooler, its contents, and a silver platter with a leg of lamb which the lackadaisical butler had left on the table. Any of those items, properly aimed, actually could have killed one of us. Screaming for help Zelda and I took cover under the heavy oak table.

Then came a hero to our rescue; that tall, spindly black butler behaved with more courage than any proper servant might have done. He broke a glass pane in the door, reached through, opened the latch, entered, and grappled with Scott. He managed to hold onto him until Zelda and I could scramble out into the night. We ran across the road to the Ring Lardner house and alerted Ring. He got us safely inside and went to look for Scott.

It took Ring nearly an hour to find him. When he did, Scott was kneeling on an unpaved road scooping up dust and cramming it into his mouth. 'What are you doing?' asked Ring. And Scott, his throat clogged with mud, gasped, 'I'm eating dirt to pay for trying to kill those two lovely girls! Those darling girls who never harmed anyone in their lives! And a swine like me tried to kill them!'

It was all very pleasant to be called 'lovely' and 'darling' and for Scott to admit swinishness, but Zelda and I had put in a very rugged evening.

Well – a lot of time had now swept by; Scott and I were safely at work in Culver City; Zelda was in a Southern asylum for the insane, where she'd been placed for her own safety. (It was there she ultimately met a horrible death in the fire that destroyed the place.)

Poor Scott had quit drinking and, from being a nuisance when tight, had taken on that apologetic humility which is often characteristic of reformed drunks. I would hear a tap on my door in the Thalberg Building and know it was Scott because nobody else ever bothered to knock before entering my office. I'd ask Scott to join whoever happened to be there; he'd enter a couple of steps, then stop. 'You people don't really want to see me!' he'd say with an embarrassing meekness. We were sorry for Scott because he seemed so alone. He never mentioned a girl friend who popped up after his death.

After a spell of uninspired conversation, Scott would conclude, 'I know you want to get rid of me so I'll go now.' Between being dangerous when drunk and eating humble pie when sober, I preferred Scott dangerous. An alcoholic is much more bearable when he's like Brendan Behan, roistering his way through to a tragic end, than for his life to fade out, as Scott's did, in one long, dull apologia.

One afternoon a few months before Scott died, he came to our house and wrote a last apology in an autograph book that's arranged according to birth dates. Scott's was September 24, and he composed the following :

> This book tells that Anita Loos
> Is a friend of Caesar, a friend of Zeus
> Of Samuel Goldwyn and Mother Goose
> Of Balanchine of the Ballet Russe
> Of Tillie the Viennese papoose (Tillie Losch)
> Of Charlie MacArthur on the loose
> Of Shanks, chiropodists – what's the use?
> Of actors who have escaped the noose
> Lots of Hollywood beach refuse
> Comics covered with Charlotte Russe
> Wretched victims of self-abuse
> Big producers all obtuse
> This is my birthday, but what the deuce
> Is that sad fact to Anita Loos
>
> – F. Scott Fitzgerald

14

Hits and Misses

WORKDAYS at the studio brought me a new companion among the writers. He was Bob Hopkins and together with Johnny Mahin and Howard Emmett Rogers we formed a maverick group which frequented a small café outside the studio, disdaining the commissary, where food was excellent, for bad coffee and stale sandwiches that were spiced with insubordination. Whenever possible, Clark Gable and Spencer Tracy joined us, as did Ted Healy, a comedian who was funnier and rowdier off screen than on. Our group was rather lacking in girls; the only ones who were welcome were Carole Lombard and Jean Harlow but, like Clark and Spence, they were generally on the set. As a free agent, I was available. The other writing females never got invited.

We called our hangout the 'Trap' and took the same delight in going there that kids do in playing hooky. L. B. tried, without success, to close the Trap, which he looked on as a hideout where we could neglect our jobs. But in many instances it was a case of our jobs neglecting *us*. We'd have preferred to be at work with Irving but he couldn't spend much time on any single project, so while waiting to be called we indulged in the fairly innocent pastimes of the Trap.

Ted Healy used to work a ploy on girls who showed up at the studio for extra jobs. Using his really superb acting talent, Ted would introduce himself as a professor attached to the personnel department; a scientist who worked along the lines of palmistry except that, instead of merely reading palms, the Professor read the entire body. 'You see, little lady,' Professor Healy explained, 'a body-reading is required for all job applicants.' Incredible as it seems, any number of those aspirants were gullible enough to place themselves in the Professor's hands. Perhaps even more incredible was the fact that Ted's only satisfaction lay in the expertise with which he carried out his work. He never took advantage of a body-reading as many an analyst is known to do while treating a gullible neurotic. When the Professor discovered an interesting case, he might call in consulting scientists; Professors Mahin, Rogers, or Hopkins (Professors Gable and Tracy had to be ruled out as recognizable). But finally news of Professor Healy's clinic filtered into L. B.'s office and he would have been fired except that, like many movie culprits, he was saved by being in the middle of a picture.

As a writer Bob Hopkins is difficult to explain. Although he was never known to put pen to paper, he had been a valued member of the MGM writing staff for years. His job was to insert gags and bits of business into any script that tended to bog down. He was always being sent for during filming to extemporize new dialogue.

The dialogue Hoppy dreamed up on-the-spot was all the more effective for having nothing to do with the action. It's certain that he never heard of Chekhov, but Hoppy used the same dramatic techniques. I remember when he was called on for a few speeches in a scene where a team of circus aerialists stood high up on a platform just before they were to crash to their deaths. 'Something dramatic!' the director ordered.

Scorning the suggestion, Hoppy offered the following :
'I saw Mabel back in Tulsa.'
'That so? How does she like being married?'

'Not too much. She's homesick.' At which point the rigging broke and, as the two crashed to the ground, Hoppy's unrelated dialogue gave the tragedy an extra shock.

Yet Hoppy himself was almost inarticulate. He spoke a sort of shorthand; a staccato that few people even tried to decipher. He was MGM's court jester, to be laughed off, but, at the same time, accorded the special affection everybody feels for a clown.

Hoppy was tall, rangy, with a shock of snow-white hair; immaculately groomed, he put up a distinguished appearance. He looked so much like Leopold Stokowski that they were sometimes mistaken for each other on the lot – until Hoppy opened up his line of gab.

One afternoon Paulette Goddard dropped into our Santa Monica home when Hoppy happened to be there, and she mistook him for the distinguished conductor. Hoppy barged over to shake Paulette's hand exclaiming in one single breath, 'Put - it - there - my - little - iffen - giffen - you're - a - whale - of - a - broad - this - day'll - go - down - in - history – If - I'd - met - the - mighty - Goddard - before - Charlie - did - you - wouldn't - be - Mrs Chaplin – Gotta - go - now - big - men - waiting - for - me !' As Hoppy breezed out, Paulette turned to me and gasped, 'Why didn't you *tell* me Stokowski was like that?'

Many of Hoppy's phrases found their way into our language. To him Jeanette MacDonald was 'the Iron Butterfly' (which came to be the standard description for the typical American beauty). When Katharine Hepburn first showed up at MGM, she was abnormally thin; 'I could toss my hat at any angle of the little broad and it would stick,' was Hoppy's comment.

Judy Garland, already a star at the age of twelve, was a compulsive weeper. There are some characters who simply cannot endure success. Judy was one of them. She loved to pace the Alley, stopping all and sundry to whimper over some imagined affront. 'Nobody loves me!' Judy would lament. She was 'persecuted' by L. B.; her family 'neglected' her; even the servants overlooked Judy. 'When I come home from work exhausted and ask for a cup of tea, the maid forgets all about it and I have to make it myself.' Judy was such a good actress that listeners were frequently impressed. Not Hoppy. He called Judy's tears 'a Hollywood bath.'

Judy's mental attitude may have been pathetic but it turned her into a great bore. And if my memories of her are few, it comes from lack of interest in a character who allowed her destiny to be ruled by petulance.

(Judy's disregard for her obligations as a star was appalling. I recall a day at the studio when mild little Vincente Minnelli [Judy's husband of the moment and the father of Liza] was waiting to direct Judy in a scene for *The Pirate*. She was late for work, as usual, and everybody, including a hundred or more extras, had been marking time since nine that morning. Finally, at noon, Vincente was summoned to the phone to learn that Judy required him to get home at once and escort her to an ice-cream parlor for a soda.)

Hoppy's life was strictly one-dimensional; the studio was as much his home as it was mine. But, not content with supplying gags, dialogue, and bits of business, Hoppy also invented plots which, unfortunately, he could never find the words to express. He would crash into Irving's office right in the midst of some important conference, to burst out with, 'Irv, you're a dunce if you don't go for this one! Gable's a gambler on a Mississippi riverboat. He's out to get a rival who's trying to louse him up. The louse gets shot and Gable decides to bury the hatchet. The big scene is a gangster funeral where Gable walks down the aisle and buries a hatchet right into the louse's goddamn big mahogany casket! When do we start to shoot it?'

Irving would say, 'Hoppy, get out!' and with no more

ado, he'd leave to go on the prowl, buttonhole another producer in the Alley, and repeat a pitch that nobody would listen to ... but me. I understood every garbled word Hoppy spoke.

Our encounter was earth-shaking for us both. Hoppy was in desperate need of a catalyst, while I had discovered one more male who needed my help.

Now, among Hoppy's numerous story ideas was one that concerned Wilson Mizner when, as a young man in San Francisco, he ran a gambling house on the Barbary Coast. Both Hoppy and I were San Franciscans too, which made for an extra bond of sympathy. Knowing Irving's admiration for Mizner, I took occasion one day to tell him Hoppy's idea. Hearing it for the first time in straightforward English, Irving was astonished. 'Do you mean our Hoppy conjured up *that* good a yarn?' he asked. I assured him that he did. 'All right,' said Irving. 'Go ahead and write it.'

Hoppy and I wrote that movie to the glory of Wilson Mizner character 'Blackie Norton.'
kids. We called our picture *San Francisco* and named the Mizner and the Frisco all three of us knew when we were.'

Its plot was unadulterated soap opera, told in an underworld setting, and it became one of MGM's most durable hits. It is still broadcast on the Late, Late TV shows. On March 12, 1972, it was listed in the TV schedule of *The New York Times*:

1:30 'San Francisco' (1936)
      Clark Gable, Jeanette MacDonald, Spencer Tracy. The works: love, opera and that super-duper earthquake. Grand show.

But just before Hoppy and I finished our final script, Irving died. His death while he was still in his thirties had been on its way a long time. For years doctors had warned Irving to slow down but his attitude had been : I'd rather die of overwork than be bored to death by inactivity.

Irving was stricken soon after he returned from a heart cure at the German spa of Bad Nauheim. It was not heart failure, per se, that brought about his death; Irving died of pneumonia as happens in many such cases. The news plunged all Hollywood into deep despair and it caused Hoppy to sentimentalize proudly, 'It wasn't the little guy's *heart* that failed him !'

With Irving gone, *San Francisco* became the most important issue in the lives of both Hoppy and me. Wilson Mizner had died in 1933 and our movie would be the means of waving both him and Irving a last good-by. But without Irving's help, we realized our movie faced grave danger. Who among the group of hobbledehoy MGM producers could understand the subtleties of a man like Wilson Mizner who was as lovable as he was monstrous?

L. B. assigned our production to Irving's greatest disciple, Bernard Hyman. But poor Bernie was a victim of that special Hollywood naïveté that's incapable of recognizing bad taste, most of all, his own. We were worried.

Our next setback turned out to be a serious brush with the board of censors. It bitterly attacked a scene in which a young priest protested our hero luring an innocent girl into a life of sin on the Barbary Coast.

BLACKIE: What's wrong with me making the little broad Queen of the Coast? I'll have Mary pose in tights and I'll plaster pictures of her on trolley cars and ash cans all over Frisco !
FATHER TIM: I'm not going to let you exploit this girl !
BLACKIE: Now, wait a minute ! *I'm going to marry her!*
FATHER TIM: You can't take a woman in marriage and then sell her immortal soul !
BLACKIE: Look Tim; I've never squawked about this God-Almighty attitude of yours from the time we were kids. But this joint

belongs to me. And the only God that's going to boss it is Blackie Norton. So you look after *your* suckers and let me look after mine!

FATHER TIM: ... Come on Mary! Come with me.

(Then, as Father Tim is leading Mary away from the joint, Blackie hauls off and floors him with a sock to the jaw.)

The administrator for the censor board, Joe Breen, sent for Hoppy and me and said grimly, 'Look here, folks. Gable is such an idol that the public may take his side when he knocks out a priest and cheer for the triumph of evil.' Hoppy's indignation made him more than usually incoherent, while I argued that our hero was to be regenerated in the long run; that the more wicked he was, the greater glory to the powers of good that would finally bring him to his knees.

'But his regeneration takes place in the last scene,' Breen protested. 'In the meantime a priest has been humiliated in a way that will bring the whole Catholic Church down on us.'

Hoppy and I loved that sequence; to cut it would emasculate the entire picture. But what could save it, now that Irving was no longer there to back us up?

The next day Hoppy and I were pacing the Alley as was our custom, this time cursing the idiotic shortsightedness of censors, when Hoppy suddenly thought of consulting the priest of the small Catholic chapel across the boulevard from the studio. Father Benedict was very movie-wise. He was often sent for to expertise on religious scenes; his confessional was frequently visited by show-biz sinners; all of which made him tremendously understanding and sympathetic to movies. Father Ben heard our problem out and racked his brains. Then presently his face lit up. 'I've thought of something that may save your precious scene,' he said.

Following Father Ben's suggestion, we went to work immediately and sketched out the scene. Next day we took it to Joe Breen. Hops proceeded to defend our scripts as if he were

Shakespeare fighting to keep the soliloquy from being tossed out of *Hamlet*.

Our new scene took place in a gymnasium where we showed that our priest could easily outbox, outslug, and outsmart Blackie. So when the two men faced their moment of truth, Tim would *purposely* allow Blackie to knock him out; thus 'presenting the other cheek' and making our priest the hero of the encounter.

I knew our solution was weak but Hoppy's fast talk finally won out. *San Francisco* was granted the go-ahead.

Bernie had snared the great Woody Van Dyke, hero of the hit film, *White Shadows in the South Seas*, to direct our movie. But no sooner did he start filming than Hoppy and I realized we again faced disaster. Van Dyke, who was capable of understanding the mentality of South Sc savages, was an oaf when it came to the subtleties of the San Francisco tenderloin.

We were horrified watching Woody direct a scene where Blackie reproves an underworld sweetheart for wearing a gaudy necklace and, indicating it, said 'Blackie told you not to wear that. It looks cheap.' Those words should have been tossed off gently and with a smile, as Wilson Mizner would have done. But Van Dyke caused our hero to jerk the necklace off the girl's throat with a brutality that cut into her skin and to bark out the dialogue in the manner of a hooligan. Not all of Gable's native charm could overcome the loutish behavior in which Van Dyke was directing him. We proceeded to Bernie's office to demand a retake. Bernie was surprised. 'Why I thought the way Woody directed that scene was swell !'

For over an hour Hoppy and I conjured up the spirit of Irving, explaining that one crass move on the part of our hero would cause the entire movie to flounder beyond recall. Bernie, bless his simple heart, finally got our viewpoint. He ordered the sequence reshot with Hoppy on the set to guide Van Dyke.

Pacing the Alley next day I said to Hoppy, 'When Irving died, he'd taken the studio to the top of a toboggan run. From now on there's only one direction MGM can go.'

'Babe, you just said a mouthful!' Hoppy declared, thus repeating a phrase that he himself might have added to the English language.

15

The Rites of Spring

March 7, 1939 – Conference with W. R.

As one of MGM's most useful scripters, I was once delegated by William Randolph Hearst to write a film for Marion Davies. The job didn't take me far afield for, although Hearst himself produced all of Marion's films, they were released by MGM. So Hearst had built a luxurious bungalow at our studio, from which he functioned. I had never felt anything but amusement over the famous publisher's mentality, but I entered his elaborate complex at MGM trembling as I had never done on an approach to Irving, whom I worshiped; evidence of the power of money over emotion.

My job would be to supply dialogue for a story of Frances Marion's called *Blondie of the Follies* and I wondered why W. R. picked me for it. When *Gentlemen Prefer Blondes* was serialized in *Harper's Bazaar*, he instructed his editor, Henry Sell, to 'stop using his magazine as a wastepaper basket!' Most likely Marion herself had asked (in her enchanting stutter), 'Will you p-p-please get Nita to write my next s-s-script.'

W. R. focused his pale, liquid eyes on me and a faint voice rose from his great bulk like the squeak of Minnie Mouse coming out of a mountain. 'Now, Nita,' he started off, 'I want you to curb your inclination toward humor because I see this story as a great romance.'

With this count against me, I dipped my pen in soothing

syrup and began an opus of which I remember nothing. However, Pauline Kael, the eminent movie analyst, recently told me that *Blondie of the Follies* still holds up quite well. Be that as it may, I finished the job to W. R.'s satisfaction and filming began with an all-star cast : Robert Montgomery, Billie Dove (then the favorite girl of billionaire Howard Hughes), Zasu Pitts, Jimmy Durante, Sidney Toler, Clyde Cook, and James Gleason. Edmund Goulding was our director.

When the rushes began to come in, W. R. and I would view them every day in his big, hollow projection room and before very long I ran into trouble. Watching a scene in which Marion was *not* on camera, W. R. rang the buzzer to stop the film and demanded, 'Why *wasn't* Muggins *in that scene?*' 'Well you see, Mr Hearst, we've got to explain an element of the plot that our heroine mustn't know about.' 'But that scene is nothing but wasted footage. Just throw it out and write one that shows Muggins doing something.' So I had to abandon the plot for a sequence of Marion picking rosebuds.

None of Marion's films ever got back their enormous cost, but I'm convinced that if W. R. had let Marion be herself, she would have ranked along with Mabel Normand as a super-box-office attraction. A pretty girl who can be a clown is rare, and Marion's off-screen antics were hilarious.

On the day when our most important love scene was to be shot, W. R. happened to be in New York and Marion strolled onto the set wearing a Charlie Chaplin tramp outfit which she'd filched from the wardrobe department. Marion twirled the cane, twitched the mustache, and ogled Bob Montgomery with an effeminacy that sent us all into stitches and drew people from sound stages all over the studio.

That romp of Marion's cost a fortune in wasted time. Eddie Goulding should have stopped her, but Marion could call any shots she fancied; besides, he was laughing more than anyone. Most Hollywood stars were tiresome egomaniacs. Not Marion. She could make one understand all the noted mistresses of history.

And regarding history, W. R. saw himself as a statesman who ranked along with Caesar, Napoleon, and Churchill. Marion agreed with W. R., as she did in everything. But when W. R. was out of earshot, Marion, inspired by his elephantine garments, called him 'Droopy Drawers' – just as she might have called Caesar 'Baldy,' or Napoleon 'Naps,' or nicknamed Churchill 'Rum Dum' because of his fondness for liquor. Marion did it not for the purpose of poking fun but with the warmest affection. She treated the whole male sex, no matter how eminent, with the tenderness one shows toward children and pets : the first requisite of a *bona fide* siren.

More money was squandered on Marion than on all the gold diggers of the fabulous Twenties. But she never had to dig. She was merely a placid target toward which riches zoomed like steel to a magnet. As a fledgling New York chorus girl, she'd been the sweetheart of another wealthy publisher, the owner of the *Brooklyn Eagle*. By the time she met Hearst, Marion had grown so used to money that it never entered her calculations. Her jewels were superb but Marion seldom wore them; when she did they seemed to lose luster, because she took so little interest in her appearance. Jewels require flaunting.

She was always surrounded by girlish houseguests and hangers-on and, since she was the last to appear in the morning, they rifled Marion's closets at will. 'In this house,' she used to say, 'the f-f-first girl up is the best d-d-dressed.'

Hearst, like any reigning monarch, occupied a number of palaces. His favorite was San Simeon. Then came a glorified Bavarian hunting lodge in the Redwood Forest of California;

there was a medieval castle in Wales; and the Beach House at Santa Monica. W. R. also kept a colony of large residences in Beverly Hills, where he could put up visiting tycoons. (Hearst and Marion happened to be occupying one of those vast cheerless houses when the famous man died.)

W. R. was obsessed with the evils of drink. The cocktail hour in any Hearst mansion was celebrated by one round of syrupy sherry; at dinner ice water took the place of wine. There was a basis for W. R.'s concern about Marion because along with her Mamma, and her sisters Rose and Reine she was as nonchalant a tippler as any descendant of old Eire.

Marion idolized every member of her slapdash family and always had them around. Sister Rose, who tried to copy Marion, had a succession of rich beaux and during one brief period was married to Baron Adlon, scion of the family that owned the Adlon Hotel in Berlin. But Rose lacked Marion's vitality. She took her bottles to bed with her. Marion's favorites in her family were Reine's son and daughter, Charlie and 'Peppy' Lederer. Her nickname fitted Peppy so well that her real one had been long forgotten.

Auntie Marion's elegant surroundings never impressed her niece and nephew. One day at San Simeon Charlie rushed into the baronial hall to sound an alarm. 'Find me a place to hide, folks! I just stuck my foot through a Goya.'

Charlie, quite early in life, started a prolific career as a screenwriter. When a musical movie was made of *Gentlemen Prefer Blondes*, he was entrusted with the scenario. The film, starring Marilyn Monroe and Jane Russell, was a huge success; but my friends had advised me not to see it. 'There's not a single scene from your book in it,' they warned. But I happened to be on board the *Île de France* when the picture was screened and, with nothing better to do, I went to see it.

I then found that Charlie had made the perfect transition of my book of which every novelist dreams. Hardly an incident of the story survived but Charlie's replacements were so much in character; his motivations so utterly correct, that the flavor of the novel remained intact. I went directly to the radio station to cable Charlie my appreciation.

Charlie's career as a brilliant scenarist and playwright has been ended by a crippling arthritis, but pain has never dimmed his spirits.

In 1969 I wrote him from New York:

Dear Charlie:
Remember me?
This is an introduction to Fred Guiles, a struggling young writer like you and I once were. He won my allegiance in a biography of Marilyn Monroe, when he summed up Arthur Miller as a phony.

Fred is about to start work on a biography of Marion and I think he deserves your attention.

Love,
Anita

Here is Charlie's reply:

Beverly Hills
March 6

Dear Anita:
This is to tell you that a writer named Fred Guiles has not shown himself on any of my horizons. This is also to tell you to expect a heavy blow on the kisser for that 'remember me' horse-manure. I regard you as part of my family and always have – an incestuous Aunt, I think.

Love as always,
Charlie

Charlie's letter was pretty badly scrawled in his own handwriting; which he went on to explain:

143

PS.: I have a secretary, but she can't type.
P.PS.: Very little work gets done.
P.P.PS: And very few letters get answered.

I visualized Charlie's secretary as a swinger and suffered a primitive reflex of jealousy. I've always been in love with Charlie Lederer a little.

As a result of W. R.'s Spartan regime, the smuggling of liquor became our daily pastime in no matter which one of his estates we were. It was fraught with suspense in which we used to dramatize W. R. as a spine-tingling bugaboo. As soon as any houseguests arrived, a servant was waiting to unpack the luggage; bottles were confiscated, not to be returned until one's departure. But a well-placed bribe generally overcame that debacle.

Life at San Simeon was filled with hazards other than getting caught red-handed with a tot of gin. The estate was stocked with wild animals, protected by signs that read 'Animals have the right of way.' At any twist in the path one might be startled by a zebra, okapi, camel, or ostrich. The more dangerous beasts were kept in cages, but we used to speculate about the bars that confined W. R.'s black panther. They looked rather spindly.

There was plenty of room outdoors for those creatures to roam because the Ranch was as big as a village. It had every convenience; a barbershop, a beauty parlor, and even its own post office. I used to go on long horseback rides high up on the cliffs with an Indian retainer. He told me he was in his seventies, was born on the Ranch, and had never set foot outside its confines.

On the shore far below the horseback trail, one could see a long complex of warehouses built to contain art objects for which W. R. couldn't find space until he got around to enlarging the castle. But that fact didn't stop him from buying, mostly by mail. I was once in London when W. R.'s English representative, Alice Head, showed me a cable from San Simeon. 'Dear Alice. There are some church bells on sale from the Cathedral in Brussels. Purchase same and have them sent at once together with a pair of male giraffes from Hamburg in good condition for breeding.'

W. R. had given Alice another mission regarding some pictures he ran across in an out-of-date art magazine. They showed a set of Irish silver, which Alice was to track down and buy. It took her a long time to trace that silver which had mysteriously disappeared. There wasn't a connoisseur in the art world who knew what had happened to it. Finally, Alice put a detective on the job and when his report came in it read : 'This item was purchased six years ago by W. R. Hearst of California.' The silver had been in packing cases ever since, hidden among the loot of a San Simeon warehouse.

In a remote area behind the castle there were a number of kennels for breeding dachshunds. Sometimes Charlie and I used to visit those most domestic of all canines, who are born to be kept in homes. They were so avid for attention that they tried to tear the iron webbing apart in their wild struggles for a pat on the head. It broke our hearts to walk away and leave them; their despairing howls could be heard almost to the castle.

One day I asked the kennel keeper why W. R. had banished those poor animals to be born, live, and die in a kennel. 'Well, you see,' he answered, 'Mr Hearst loves dachshunds.' And that was true; Marion's constant companion was a miniature dachshund. So W. R.'s cruelty could only have been caused by one of those blind spots which afflict the eyes of the abnormally rich.

Castles are not supposed to be very livable, but San Simeon achieved total discomfort. Charlie once remarked, 'If you're offered the choice of a second-class hotel, you'd do well to skip San Simeon!' The main structure had been carted over from Europe piecemeal and reassembled on a crag overlooking the Pacific. Its chambers were frosty. The innumerable bedrooms were equipped with fireplaces of great antiquity, from which smoke poured as from the gaping mouths of dragons. Small electric heaters were dotted about but they couldn't begin to warm those vaulted Gothic chambers.

In the morning I would huddle under the plush canopy of a seventeenth-century bed, trying to summon enough courage to get up. Once you had made a shivering way to the bathroom, there was abundant hot water but again frustration. The bathtub was of marble, which is impossible to heat. In a tub filled with hot water, you sat as though on a cake of ice. To stand under a warm shower gave you chilblains.

Promptly at seven o'clock the entire Hearst Court had to report at the breakfast table and to the guests, who might number twenty or more, it was sheer torture. As a consequence, the table-talk was spotty. To give a slight idea of its caliber, a snip like me generally occupied the seat of honor next to W. R. He spoke very little, so I used to take refuge in praising Marion's movies, which may be the reason why I sat next to him.

However, I did encounter a glint of humor in W. R. one time in New York. It was during the early stages of his romance with Marion. She and I had been seated to W. R.'s right and left at dinner in a hideaway he kept at the old Beaux Arts apartment building. Now it so happened that I'd been asked by W. R.'s wife, Millicent, to dine the very following evening at the legitimate Hearst home on Riverside Drive. When dinner was announced I was embarrassed to find myself again seated next to W. R. But as I took my place he observed with the first twinkle I ever saw

146

in those pale eyes of his, 'Well, Nita, we seem to be meeting under rather different circumstances, don't we?'

From time to time, people of real importance joined W. R. at San Simeon, bent on garnering some Hearst publicity. But they were seldom able to improve the general tone of conversation, which might frequently be lowered by the presence of W. R.'s chief editorial writer, Arthur Brisbane. I recall a discussion between Hearst and Brisbane during an alarming period of World War I. 'I have discovered a weapon that can wipe out our enemy's trenches in a matter of hours,' Brisbane pontificated. 'Tell us about it, Arthur!' squeaked W. R. 'Well – recently I visited a placer mine in Northern California, and the idea came to me that it would be quite easy to flush the Germans out of their trenches with water gushing from giant hoses.' Nodding approval, W. R. said, 'You must communicate that to the War Department, Arthur.'

I might have piped up, But Northern California is full of waterfalls, Mr Brisbane. Where would water come from on the Western Front?' I kept my mouth shut, for who was I to contradict a man whose every thought was gobbled up by Hearst.

On another occasion, Brisbane delivered himself of yet another giant thought. 'The next time war seems imminent, Chief, I've thought up a plan to divert it. We'll get the Hearst syndicate to organize an international beauty contest that will completely take people's minds off warfare.' (N.B. Mr Brisbane couldn't have been joking. He had no sense of humor.)

Evenings in any Hearst domain were identical. As soon as dinner was over came the inevitable movie. We might have enjoyed using it as a cue for wisecracks but W. R. frowned on disrespect of that kind. As soon as the movie was over W. R. took Marion off to bed. Nothing could have been more domestic.

A typical rumor used to go the rounds that concerned Marion, W. R., and a little French actress, Simone Simon. She had entered the Hollywood scene for a while, appeared in a few undistinguished films, and then returned home (where, incidentally, she is now a chic and glamorous Parisienne). With Mademoiselle Simon's departure from Hollywood, a rumor developed that she was Marion's daughter by W. R. Apparently the only basis for the mistake was that, in the minds of film fans, the name Simone Simon bore a vague resemblance to that of the San Simeon Ranch.

W. R. was one of the few very rich people I ever knew who was infinitely generous and thoughtful. When he invited a guest, every expense of the visit was prepaid. We girls were also advised by Marion to go window-shopping along the vitrines in hotel lobbies. 'If you s-s-see anything you like,' Marion would tell us, 'just ch-ch-charge it to your room. When the bills are p-p-paid, nobody l-l-looks at them.'

One afternoon in Paris, Marion and I went forth to stroll. Walking along the Champs-Élysées, we came to the Renault automobile showroom. While pressing our noses against the window, Marion suggested 'Let's g-g-go in.'

She sought out a salesman and, gesturing toward a limousine on display, said 'I'll t-t-take eight of those.' Thinking he'd misunderstood, the salesman asked, 'Did Mademoiselle say eight?' 'Y-y-yes, that's r-r-right.' The salesman appeared so nonplussed that I came to the rescue. 'They're to be billed to Mr William Randolph Hearst.' The magic name was a convincer. Next day, eight Renault limousines were delivered to the hotel, from which our group took off gaily for Bad Nauheim.

That sort of heyday, alas, couldn't go on forever. But when a time finally came that W. R.'s massive extravagance was about to cost him his entire empire, Marion pledged everything she owned to come to his rescue – jewels, California real estate, New York skyscrapers, the Ritz Tower Apartments, and the Hotel Warwick. Actually those were no great sacrifices; Marion's one real luxury was laughter, which was built-in and for free.

I happened to be with Marion at the Beach House when a team of Hearst's New York lawyers came to Santa Monica in an effort to rescue him from bankruptcy. While the meeting was in session Marion said 'Let's l-l-listen at the keyhole and hear what's g-g-going to happen to "Droopy Drawers"' We listened and heard the complicated plan by which his brilliant legal counsel saved the Hearst empire from ever again being threatened and allowed Hearst to go on spending and Marion laughing clear up to the end.

Marion had a pet joke for each one of us. Mine was that I was her illegitimate child by Calvin Coolidge. I can let Marion tell about it herself.

San Simeon
December 25, 1941

My Darling Little Anita (by Coolidge),
Your lovely bubble bath gives me wonderful ideas. Maybe I could strive for Gable? No. Cooper? No. Tracy? Maybe. I guess I'll stay home and keep clean and smell good to myself.

Millions of thanks, darling, for making a clean, upstanding citizen of me.

Affectionately,
Marion

Nothing could ever have separated W. R. and Marion except death. On New Year's Eve of 1950, Marion led a small group of us that included Charlie Lederer and Louella Parsons to the cheerless residence in Beverly Hills occupied by W. R. and Marion at the moment. Before entering The Presence, Marion warned us: 'He can't t-t-talk so don't ask h-h-how he is. Just m-m-make conversation as usual – you know, b-b-be idiotic.'

Trying our hardest to seem nonchalant, we filed into a large, sparsely furnished bedroom where W. R. lay inert. But as we spoke those large, liquid eyes shifted to each one of us. Their expression registered mild interest in such items as, 'You're going to love Louella's new porch furniture, Mr Hearst.' After a few pearls of thought we filed out, vastly shaken, and it took Sam Spiegel's annual New Year's Eve wing-ding to revive our spirits.

By the next New Year's Eve Marion was alone at long last. She never even got to tell 'Droopy Drawers' good-by. The Hearst family spirited his body away while Marion was under deep sedation.

Disrespectful as most of us were about Hearst, there was an area in which I never underestimated him. W. R. was a very great lover. Eminent statesmen, warriors, artists, and intellectuals crowd the encyclopedias. But of great lovers there are very few. Looking back over the many years I was close to W. R. and Marion, I could only view their relationship as pastoral. And, to counteract any idea that the ideal lover must be young and sightly, let me mention a group of classic sketches by the great Picasso in which ravishing little girls are pursued by idyllic old boys with the greatest possible homage to both Art and Beauty. The Rites of Spring . . .

16

MGM Makes Room for a Genius

ONE momentous day, during the time Mr E. and I lived in New York, I got a letter that was to have lifelong consequences.

> Congress Hotel
> Chicago

14-May-1926
Dear Miss Anita Loos,
I have no excuse for writing to you – no excuse, except that I was enraptured by the book, have just hugely enjoyed the play, and am to be in America so short a time that I have no leisure to do things in the polite and tortuous way. My wife and I are to be in New York for about a fortnight from Monday 17th onwards and it would be a very great pleasure – for us at any rate – if we could arrange a meeting with you during that time. Please forgive my impatience and accept the sincere admiration which is its cause and justification.

> Yours very sincerely,
> Aldous Huxley

Soon after the Huxleys arrived in New York they came to tea at our apartment. When first meeting Aldous one was struck by his enormous majesty; he was a giant in height with the look of an archangel drawn by William Blake. And his myopic eyes made him appear to be focusing on things above and beyond what ordinary mortals saw.

Maria was a tiny brunette, who never lost the figure of the ballerina she had studied to be as a girl. A native of

Belgium, she was among a group of children sent to London to escape the Germans in Belgium at the beginning of World War I.

Maria became the teen-age bride of Aldous when every eminent British bluestocking was in love with the handsome young genius. Having danced off with their idol never endeared Maria to such man-eating sirens as Edith Sitwell and Lady Ottoline Morrell.

After years of trying out various climates in Europe, the Huxleys and their son Matthew, settled in Los Angeles where the dry air was agreeable to Aldous's never robust lungs. Then, after smog invaded Los Angeles, they took refuge in the nearby desert and, while living in the little village of Pear Blossom, Aldous's vision improved so much that he was able to drive his car on the lonely desert roads. He even took to sketching the surrounding landscapes.

Soon after settling in Los Angeles, the Huxleys collected a group of friends; among them Edwin Hubble, the distinguished astronomer and theorist of the expanding universe and his brilliant wife, Grace, Gerald Heard, Christopher Isherwood, Krishnamurti, Charlie Chaplin, and Paulette Goddard.

Maria Huxley was a living definition of the word 'fey.' Her existence sparkled with fascinating idiocies. Because she seemed to live on air and water, Maria's attitude toward food made her a very peculiar housewife. Not that she didn't earnestly put her mind to the job.

I recall a menu she worked out with the aid of a calorie counter, to include all the nutrients for an evening meal. It consisted of a platter of string beans at room temperature surrounded by cold sliced bananas. When Aldous diplomatically insisted on leading us off to the Farmers' Market for a banquet, Maria's wide blue eyes grew misty with chagrin.

But she never bored us; never failed us as a conversation piece; and always joined the laughter at her own expense.

At their son Matthew's sixteenth birthday party, Maria served a group of ravenous teen-agers with portions of roast chicken that were extremely skimpy because she had cut off and thrown away the drumsticks.

Using an Elizabethan pet name by which they addressed each other, Aldous asked, 'But Sweetins, why didn't you cook the drumsticks?' 'Because, Sweetins, they looked so gross in comparison with their dainty little wings.' The Farmers' Market again proved a lifesaver and Matthew had a happy birthday, after all.

Along with her eccentricities, Maria had virtues that made her a true helpmeet. She was Aldous's best-loved companion, his secretary-typist, and in Hollywood she drove the family car. Best of all, she protected Aldous from the swarms of pests and ridiculous disciples that attach themselves to a great man.

For years our lives ran along the most pleasant lines. Every Sunday we went for long walks on the beach or through the many firebreaks that criss-cross the dry hills surrounding Hollywood. Those walks set us apart from other Southern Californians, who are so dependent on wheels that to use the feet for transportation makes one suspect. One evening we were on a stroll in Beverly Hills when two policemen in a patrol car stopped to order us off the sidewalk or they'd take us to the station. That near-arrest greatly amused Aldous as a measure of California's *Kultur*.

Aldous's erudition was staggering; I never learned how many languages he knew, but one day I found him in his office at MGM reading Persian. No cut-and-dried intellectual, he had a childlike curiosity about everything. He was fascinated by the crackpot population of Southern California and its weird religious cults : the 'Four Square Gospel' of Aimee

Semple McPherson; a cult called 'The Great I am,' and the mass wriggling on the floor of the Holy Rollers. Aldous was criticized in England for 'gullibility,' but he was a scientist whose subject was human behavior, and to overlook such oddities as Aimee Semple McPherson would have been as negligent as an entomologist who disregarded the gnat.

Aldous and Marie both clung to a childish love for picnics, and one excursion they organized might have taken place in *Alice in Wonderland*. Among us were several Theosophists from India, the most prominent being Krishnamurti. The ladies wore saris which looked rather strange under the circumstances, but the remainder of our party was dressed in beat-up old clothes. Nobody would have recognized Greta Garbo, who, to protect herself from recognition, wore a sloppy pair of men's trousers and a battered hat with a brim that hid her face. Paulette Goddard, then Mrs Chaplin, made a concession to glamour in a Mexican peasant outfit with colored yarn woven into her braids. As always, she looked savagely romantic. (Paulette's combination of beauty and erudition has always been catnip to geniuses. There have been two among her four husbands : Charlie Chaplin and Erich Remarque. Aldous had developed a little sneaker for Paulette which is rather given away by the heroine of *After Many a Summer Dies the Swan*. Her physical description fits Paulette to a T; she even wears the white sharkskin tennis garments affected by Mrs Chaplin.) Bertrand Russell, who was a Hollywood visitor, looked like a pixie on a spree. So did Charlie Chaplin and Christopher Isherwood. Aldous himself might have been the giant from some second-rate circus. The only 'normal' member of our group was Matthew Huxley, who looked like any grubby teen-ager.

Krishnamurti and his followers, forbidden to eat from vessels that had been contaminated by animal substance, were weighed down with pots and pans in which to cook their lunch. Their kitchenware made quite a clatter. Greta, on a strict diet, carried a supply of vegetables which were, as yet, in bunches. Paulette, to whom no occasion is festive without champagne and caviar, brought them along in thermos containers.

Our various cars had met on Sunset Boulevard and we proceeded in a parade to look for a spot where it would be safe to build a camp fire, always a hazard because of the brush fires which constantly plague Southern California (except when it is plagued by devastating floods). At length we found a spot which was ideal for safety : the dusty bottom of the Los Angeles River, which during the rainy season is a raging torrent and the remainder of the year is drier than a desert.

The Indian delegation set about to boil their rice, but while we were unpacking the other picnic fare we were rudely shocked by a gruff voice demanding, 'What the hell's going on here?' As we reacted, stunned into silence, there hove into view a sheriff, or some reasonable facsimile, with a gun in his hand.

'Don't anybody in this gang know how to read?' he asked Aldous. Aldous meekly allowed he could read, but he still didn't understand the man until he pointed out a sign we hadn't noticed. It read 'No Trespassing.'

Aldous politely explained we were not going to desecrate the Los Angeles River (already strewn with rusty cans, pop bottles, and assorted rubbish) and said if we might be permitted to eat lunch, we'd clean up and leave the river bed neat and tidy.

Aldous's plea was getting nowhere; the sheriff, glowering and fingering his gun, said 'Get going! And that means now!'

Feeling responsibility as our host, Aldous decided to play a trump card; to introduce a few awesome names : Greta

Garbo, Paulette Goddard, and Charlie Chaplin. The sheriff squinted his measly little eyes at them.

'Don't give me that!' he snarled. 'I seen them stars in the movies and none of 'em belong in this outfit. Get out of here, you tramps, or I'll arrest the whole slew of you.'

So we folded our tents like the Arabs, and guiltily stole away.

We were always trying to delve into Nature, of which most Southern Californians want no part. I recall another jaunt in which Garbo was our girl guide. Greta had discovered a spring on a remote hilltop where the Indians were said to have bathed in early days. 'I'm sure the water is medicinal,' said Greta, a dyed-in-the-wool ecologist long before ecology became a fad. We all trooped up a barren hill and at its top found the spring; its water dribbled through a rusty pipe into a battered old tin bathtub. But lazing away in the tub was a very hairy tramp who ordered us off his premises in much worse language than our hard-hearted sheriff's.

There was one occasion when Aldous's interest in flim-flam paid off. He took a group of us to a little fish restaurant on the Santa Monica pier. During dinner, he spotted a hand-writing analyst plying her trade in a booth next to a shooting gallery. Among our group were Paulette and Charlie Chaplin and, after dinner, Aldous suggested that Charlie write a few words on a scrap of paper and let him present it to the analyst. (Charlie was to remain out of sight because he might be recognized.)

The analyst studied Charlie's handwriting gravely and then asked Aldous in reproval, 'Are you playing a trick on me, sir?' 'Why, no,' Aldous answered. 'Then the writer of this must have held the paper against a wall or in a cramped position.' 'No, Madam, he wrote it on a table quite normally. What made you think otherwise?' 'Because if this specimen is authentic, it was written by a God-given genius.'

Aldous became a devotee of the handwriting expert, who turned out to be a lady of breeding and an authority in her field. The reason for her shoddy place of business was a heart condition which required the oxygen one inhales close to the ocean.

On Sundays the Huxleys always lunched with us; other regulars were Charlie Chaplin and Paulette, when she was Mrs Chaplin. Edwin and Grace Hubble often came over from Pasadena. Edwin was in charge of the Mount Wilson Observatory, where he worked out his epoch-making theory of the expanding universe.

From time to time we entertained such cultured visitors as H. G. Wells and Bertrand Russell. One day Ruth and Garson Kanin were among us, and a paragraph in a local gossip column reported, 'It is an extraordinary experience to lunch at the Emersons' with intellectuals like Aldous Huxley, Edwin Hubble, Bertrand Russell, and H. G. Wells. and listen to Ruth Gordon talk.'

When the growing industries of Los Angeles began to darken the air with smog, the Huxleys retreated to the cliffs that overlook the Pacific in Santa Monica. So far, so good. The view was breathtaking but the Huxley house gloried in objects which could have been assembled in no other culture of the world. On entering the hall one was greeted by a larger-than-life facsimile of a gorilla which had once been used to advertise the movie King Kong. In his hairy grip a fairly nude Fay Wray was wriggling to escape, while Kong looked around for a comfortable spot to commit rape. A bar of dowdy grandeur was graced by tortured motifs cut out with a fret saw, and multi-colored lights revolved and shed their radiance on a stuffed crocodile. Aldous might have pitched the entire décor into the cellar, 'But,' said he, 'why dispense with so unique a source of amazement in a world filled with tedium?'

During World War II, Aldous instituted an unspoken agreement not to discuss the war. On the day that Paris was occupied by the Nazis, a group came to dine at our house. When Aldous arrived his face was dead-white and bore the expression of someone who was peering into hell; but the talk was mostly some sort of scientific discussion between Aldous and Edwin Hubble. Nobody mentioned Paris.

Incredible as it may appear, there were times when I felt a little superior to Aldous. He once came to tell me that, stanchly as he had remained apart from the movie industry, he was now tempted to try for a job in it. The Battle of Britain was on in full force; it had curtailed his income and increased his obligations. Did I think he might possibly make good in the movies? Amused at his humility, I told Aldous nothing could be easier than to find him a job. Next day at the studio, I learned that the outline of *Pride and Prejudice* had been finished and it was ready for dialogue. I informed the producer, Hunt Stromberg, that the great British writer was available, and he immediately set up an appointment to see Aldous the next day.

Soon after their interview my phone rang. Aldous was calling, with Maria on an extension, and their mood was one of gloomy resignation.

'I'm sorry,' Aldous said, 'but I realize now that I can't take that movie job.'

I wanted to know why not.

'Because it pays twenty-five hundred dollars a week,' he answered in deep distress. 'I simply cannot accept all that money to work in pleasant surroundings while my family and friends are going hungry and being bombed in England.'

'But Aldous,' I asked, 'why can't you accept the money and send it to England?'

There was a moment of silence and then Maria spoke up. 'Anita, what ever would we do without you?'

'The trouble with a genius like Aldous,' I told her, 'is that he just isn't very smart.'

Aldous accepted the job and ultimately joined the writing staff at MGM, where every assignment proved, in one way or another, to amaze him. Because of his scientific knowledge, Aldous was delegated to do the technical research on the story of the discovery of radium by Marie and Pierre Curie. Their venture was as much a love affair as a scientific achievement, and a 'natural' for films. The romantic pair were to be played by Greer Garson and Walter Pidgeon.

Aldous sent for a complete file of French newspapers that covered the period of the discovery of radium. One day he phoned me excitedly from his office. 'Come down here right away! I've got something amazing to show you.' I enjoyed being amazed as much as he did and lost no time.

Spread out on Aldous's desk were a number of newspaper clippings on an aspect of the Curie romance we'd never heard about. A certain journalistic sleuth had uncovered a 'love nest' in a shoddy Paris hotel where Marie Curie held trysts with her husband's young assistant. There was even a photograph of the room, bare of furniture except for a double bed. But over the headboard there hung a large framed portrait of, guess who? *Pierre Curie!*

Naturally MGM couldn't use that episode in its film but later Aldous made it the basis for his most successful stage play, *The Genius and the Goddess*, for which I supplied him with a collaborator; my dear friend Beth Wendell.

Another of Aldous's assignments was almost as amazing. He was informed that Greta Garbo wished to talk with him about a project she had in mind. To be sent for by Garbo was indeed an event. Although we were sometimes with her socially, Greta seldom came to the studio; nobody knew where she lived or even had her phone number, except her one confidante, Salka Viertel. All professional matters had to be conducted with Salka and *without* Garbo.

Aldous's conference with Garbo took place in her dressing room, from which he came straight to me to report. 'The Divine One wants me to write her a film on Saint Francis of Assisi,' he announced. 'What a great idea, Aldous! She'd be heartbreaking as Clare!' 'So I told her,' Aldous chuckled. 'But Greta wants to play Saint Francis!'

'You're fooling!' 'Not at all! I tried to talk her out of the idea; told her the role posed an insurmountable problem because it is universally known that the Saint wore a beard.' 'Oh yes,' Greta had agreed, 'but the make-up department can easily make me one!' (I don't know who scotched that Garbo movie.)

To my viewpoint, Aldous's sense of humor outshone all other facets of his tremendously complex nature. It even came into play at the time when one of those hellish Southern California brush fires had destroyed the home where Aldous then lived with Laura, whom he had married about a year after Maria's death. He and Laura had scarcely escaped with their lives, but Aldous's manuscripts, Maria's diaries with their record of the eventful years they spent together, Aldous's priceless collection of letters from great people of his day, and a library that had taken years to assemble, were all reduced to ashes.

I was in New York when I heard of this disaster and hurried to phone Aldous my sympathy. 'It was a hideous experience,' he exclaimed. I could visualize his quizzical smile when he added, 'But it did make me feel extraordinarily clean!'

I fear I never appreciated Aldous's more serious interests; at times when he discussed such matters as LSD and even ESP, I kept my mouth shut, out of humility.

I shall always remember Aldous as smiling. A birthday present he once sent me was a bottle of Schiaparelli's 'Shocking' perfume (long since evaporated) in a box made in the shape of a book. On the flyleaf Aldous wrote: 'For Anita, one of the few books that doesn't stink.'

17

What Killed Jean Harlow

ONE afternoon while Hoppy and I were having coffee in the Trap, he thought of a colorful character on which to base a movie for Jean Harlow. She would play the daughter of a horsetrader, born and raised in an environment of race tracks. The locale would be Saratoga, which would also be the title of the film.

We told our idea to our producer, Bernie Hyman, who said, 'That sounds like a possibility. Go ahead!'

When our story was ready to be put into script form, Bernie hired a jockey from the Santa Anita track to supply a proper vernacular for the dialogue. (Our pal Bernie was a stickler for authenticity. When he produced *The Great Waltz* he rented a Stradivari violin at $1000 a day for an actor who couldn't have played a bazooka.)

Our jockey was a wizened little man of about forty who bore out my contention that jockeys are among the most civilized men in the world. Sitting over coffee in the Trap, he gave me a lesson I couldn't have gotten in a Yale drama course.

'Look, honey,' he said, 'if you use jockey terms in your dialogue, you'll be writing a movie for jockeys and just between the two of us, folks who spend their time with horses don't care very much about films. Write your dialogue in your own words and it'll sound okay even to a jockey.'

The filming of *Saratoga* had been completed except for its final scene, when Jean was suddenly taken with what seemed to be a mild sort of ailment that kept her home. Jack Conway started 'shooting around her,' as they say in films.

One afternoon, a group of us were sitting in Bernie's outer office : there were Clark Gable; Bernie's secretary, Goldie; and the switchboard operator, who happened to be a boy. We began to talk of Jean and to wonder what her ailment was. No use asking her Ma because Ma didn't believe in the existence of disease. 'Probably drunk again,' said Clark, making a pretty stupid joke because Jean was not given to drinking when on the job.

'Let's call up and ask her when she's coming back,' I suggested. The boy at the switchboard got through to Jean's house, talked briefly to a servant, and then hung up.

'They've taken Jean to Cedars of Lebanon!' he said with apprehension. We all began to be disturbed; because for Ma to allow her precious baby to be hospitalized was a pretty radical move. Clark suggested we call the hospital. The call went through. Presently, the boy's face turned deathly white and the receiver clattered onto the desk. We knew what had happened before he told us. 'Jean's dead !'

Then was the studio thrown into dismay; Jean had earned millions for MGM and stood to make many more. L. B. took the tragedy as a personal affront, but just the same he issued a humanitarian edict. 'The next time one of our valuable properties gets sick, the studio's got to find out what's the matter.'

Jean's funeral at Forest Lawn was an orgy of grief, with mobs of weeping fans, monitored by the police. L. B. sent a heart of red roses five feet tall pierced by a golden arrow. But those of us who were close to the bier were more impressed when one of Jean's former costars, Bill Powell, strode up to place a single white rose on her breast.

After it was too late, the studio tried to find some reason for Jean's death. She'd always enjoyed the best of health.

When stricken, her symptoms seemed to be merely those of fatigue. One theory was that overexposure to sun might have brought on a fatal uremia. But the doctors and nurses the reason Jean's platinum hair looked so natural, was as sensitive as an albino's. But then, she never went into the sunlight unless protected by long sleeves, a high neckline, a big floppy hat, and a parasol. Ma *could* be relied on for that !

Another notion was that excessive use of bleach might have brought on a fatal uremia. But the doctors and nurses who had hovered over Jean at the hospital agreed on one thing; she had refused to put up a fight. And this fact bolstered a theory of my own on what caused Jean to die.

Unlike Marilyn Monroe, Jean was not a narcissist. To her, sex had come to be an incessant matter-of-talk that would have bored Messalina. She recognized her looks as an accident of birth. The platinum hair that brought her to fame was a nuisance because she had to spend an hour in the make-up department every second day for its roots to be touched up. Jean's attitude toward clothes was that of a small boy who balks at being dressed up. I never knew her to go shopping. Jean's mother bought everything for her. Jean would slip into a new dress without bothering to glance in the mirror. Why bother? She always looked the same ... terrific.

So all right! She *was* terrific. But to whom? To her distant public, to a trio of husbands that included a Kansas City playboy, a German psycho, and a mild little MGM cameraman, all of them the dull type of gentlemen who prefer blondes.

Between those three disastrous episodes which Jean philosophically called 'marriages of *in*convenience,' she lived with her mother, who was her replica in looks, platinum hair and all, except in a more opulent form. Ma was married to a florid gentleman of Italian descent named Marino Bello, who was equipped with all the gigolo tricks to make a female happy. But Marino was given to writing Jean unwelcome love notes that had to be kept secret from her mother.

Jean was always lonely; she longed to find companionship in a lover, one with wit enough to respond to her compulsive wisecracks. But very early in life she realized she was doomed to failure. Irving, for instance, found her nothing more than a booby trap for male stupidity.

Because Jean granted so little importance to sex, she could be thoughtlessly cruel at times. Soon after she married Paul Bern he took Jean and me to a football match. That day Paul made a great issue of his bride's comfort; supplying her with a cushion, a lap robe, a hot dog, a bottle of soda. Finally, he asked if he could get her anything more. Jean indicated a husky fullback down on the field and said, 'Yes, Daddy. Get me that one!' Jean and I laughed, having no inkling how the joke must have tortured her impotent bridegroom.

But the same impotence that could so easily be a joke ultimately caught Jean up in the most horrifying experience a girl in Hollywood ever had to go through.

Bern adored Jean as abjectly as only a German psycho might. But expecting no return of his ardor, he had had to woo her with arguments unrelated to sex. He maintained that, as a producer, he'd devote all his talents to her career.

He was good and kind and gentle and Jean had had too many experiences with men who were weak, selfish, or evil. At that very moment, she was living under the same roof with one of the worst, her own mother's husband. 'It'll be a relief to get away from the rat before Mom finds him out,' Jean told me.

In short, for Jean to marry someone as respectful as Paul Bern seemed a very bright thing to do. 'Paul's so sweet,' Jean said to me, 'he'd cut out his own heart before he'd ever do me in.'

And then, even *Bern* did Jean in.

He may have counted on his marriage producing a miracle and that, with an inspiration like Jean, he could conquer his impotence. Well – he couldn't.

As time went on, the poor man tried to assuage his guilt by practices which Jean was too normal to accept. But she understood; didn't blame her husband; assured him how little sex meant to her. Jean's tolerance went even further; 'Just do anything you like, sweetheart,' she said, 'but count me out of those sessions. Find yourself someone else. I won't object; I'll understand.'

Still putting up a bluff at manhood, Bern agreed. And then one evening, to bolster his pretenses, he told Jean of a rendezvous he'd made. When he was leaving for his date she kissed him tolerantly and wished him good night.

Next morning Jean found a note under her bedroom door. It said, in essence, 'I hope you'll understand that last night was a farce. Now I'm yours forever. Paul.'

Puzzled, Jean went to ask for an explanation. Bern lay sprawled on his bedroom floor in a pool of blood. There was a bullet hole in his head and his squat, fat body, so ill-equipped for marriage, was shamefully naked. Paul Bern's suicide was the very apotheosis of masochism, for he had killed himself while looking in a full-length mirror.

Jean's role in that tragedy of Beauty-and-the-Beast must have destroyed the last small vestige of faith she may have had in men. But then, prior to filming *Saratoga*, she had co-starred in a picture with William Powell. Bill had all the qualities which Jean despaired of ever finding in a sweetheart. He was a gentleman – urbane, witty, and charming. It began to flash on her consciousness that sex need not be snide and degrading. She turned her full battery of feminine charms on Bill.

But Bill happened to have been the victim of another

dynamic blonde. He had been married to Carole Lombard whose incredible glamour made him feel inferior, reduced his ego practically to the situation of a Paul Bern. Bill needed some Little-Miss-Nobody in order to regain his polarity. So he walked out on Jean and, about three years after her death, he finally discovered just what he'd been looking for; a blonde as cute and pretty as Jean but with the one virtue Jean lacked, anonymity. Ball married his charmer without more ado and they began to live happily ever after.

After Bill's rejection, Jean seemed to lose interest in everything; and, when stricken, she refused to put up a fight. It was as if Jean took advantage of a minor ailment to escape from life. Her mother's reason was saved by her faith; she never admitted that Jean was gone.

The filming of *Saratoga* was completed with an actress in a platinum wig substituting for Jean. The camera angles featured Clark fullface, with the substitute's back to the camera.

Saratoga confounded all the experts who claimed that Jean's tragedy would keep people out of the theaters. The movie stacked up a fortune which, to L. B. at least, made for a happy ending.

To become a star an actress must be sensitive. A letter Jean wrote me after the Bern tragedy could only have been written by a woman of warmth and sensitivity.

Anita Dear,
Could I but make you know the depths of gratitude I have for your most wonderful letter with its expressions of loyalty, friendship, and understanding. Without friends, I could not have gone on. Please know I shall always treasure your wonderful faith in me and will never disappoint you.

Devotedly and gratefully,
Jean

Jean had all the sensitivity required of a star. But to remain one, an actress also has to be an egomaniac. Jean didn't have enough ego to survive, and so the movies' greatest femme fatale simply died of sex starvation.

18

A Sick Script Needs a Doctor

SOME of those MGM directors could be totally ignorant of the life they were trying to depict. Worldliness was a scarce commodity in Hollywood and because I'd gotten around a bit, Irving sometimes used me as a trouble shooter.

There was an occasion when he asked me to take a look at a set where Sidney Franklin was directing a grand ballroom scene. 'It's supposed to be the last word in Victorian elegance,' Irving said, 'but Sidney's got a Dowager Duchess wearing a very ordinary afternoon outfit. I'm no authority on ladies' clothes,' he added, 'but if you'll talk to Sid he may listen.'

I went down to the set where I found that Sidney's actresses were all wearing opulent ball gowns except an elderly Duchess, who was in gray alpaca with a high collar and long sleeves. Getting Sidney aside, I asked the reason for that informal costume. He was annoyed. 'I've had a dozen fights over that dress!' he grumbled. 'People don't realize that a director's job is to deal with *character*, and in my book, no respectable old lady would wear a low-necked gown!'

I was only able to convince Sidney by sending to the research department for a picture of Queen Victoria *en décolleté*. Although deflated by such royal nudity, he finally sent his Duchess off to the wardrobe department for a proper evening dress. Due to the pioneer quality of those days in Hollywood, many a high-salaried director would have been lucky, elsewhere, to get a job as a hardware clerk.

Sometimes Irving put me to work as a 'script doctor' on ailing plots. One such assignment was to go over the final script of *The Merry Widow* with Ernst Lubitsch. No matter who wrote Ernst's scenarios, he himself put in the 'Lubitsch touches' that made his films unique.

Although Ernst had none of the shortcomings of a Sidney Franklin, Irving was always worried about his tendency to neglect the human element in a story. Any love scene Ernst directed might just be warming up when his camera would zoom away from the sweethearts to focus on a pair of fancy bedroom slippers, the hero's pearl-buttoned spats, or an ornate piece of bric-a-brac. I was instructed to keep reminding Ernst that his plot concerned the human heart and not the prop department.

Ernst grudgingly accepted my aid on the script, which was to star Jeanette MacDonald and Maurice Chevalier; but as soon as work got under way, I found him obsessed by an idea of the Widow owning a pair of poodles, one snow-white and the other coal-black; a gimmick that kept interrupting the love story. In an attempt to get on with the romance, I came up with a self-conscious line of dialogue that finally won Ernst's approval; our hero would say to the Widow, 'You have brought a ray of *moon* light into my life!'

Later, when I sat with Irving in the projection room and listened to Chevalier speak that phony line, Irving winced and said 'There goes our love story!' I never told my boss I was to blame. However, the great movie public, which had accepted Cecil B. De Mille as the high priest of *savoir-faire*, was entranced by the bag of tricks in Ernst's *Merry Widow*. It was a big hit.

Anent Ernst's own sophistication, I recall an afternoon in Irving's office when he sat with Irving and me, squirming as he told a tale of woe. He was in the throes of being black-mailed by a flashy *mittel*-European femme fatale with whom he'd had a whirl on a trip home to Berlin. But she had trailed Ernst back to Hollywood, where she produced some copies of his love letters and now threatened to publish the originals unless Ernst came through with fifty thousand hard-earned dollars.

Looking at him quizzically, Irving asked 'And what's *in* those letters?' Ernst sheepishly handed them over. After reading a line or two, Irving gave them back. 'Look, my friend, if you can keep *these* out of print for fifty thousand, you've got a bargain. *Grab it!*' So that great European man-of-the-world paid up, just like any gullible American dope.

Once I was required to tackle a rush job that had to do with Clare Boothe's *The Women*. When Irving sent for me, I found him with George Cukor, who was going to direct the picture. Both were in a mild state of panic.

At that time the most innocent jokes about sex were banned and Clare's script had just been returned by the Censor Board with a great number of her laugh-lines blue-penciled. Filming was to start the next morning and Irving informed me I was to sit beside George on the set and ad lib some 'clean' jokes as the cameras rolled. (Seeing that there are plenty of laughs in the ordinary bitchiness of women, it was no hard job.)

George was one of the few really creative directors at MGM. He had chosen Paulette Goddard for a role in *The Women* when her exceptional allure had already earned her Charlie Chaplin for a husband, a lavish estate as a home, a mass of priceless jewels, and her own custom-built Rolls to bring her to work. But when it came to directing Paulette, George told her, 'Look, kid, just forget those female tricks of yours and try to give me the best imitation you can of *Spencer Tracy!*' Being smart, Paulette instantly got the idea. So, in spite of her youth and lack of training, she turned in the performance of a seasoned character actress.

George also had a genius for casting. He could detect hidden qualities in an actress that would make a star of her when, except for George Cukor, she might never have been heard of.

There was one minor role in *The Women* for which George, against Irving's advice, insisted on using a dancer who'd never spoken a line professionally. Even the girl's beauty was yet to be discovered. True, she was graceful, as she belonged to a Spanish family that worked in vaudeville as a dancing group. But she suffered grave imperfections. Her mouse-colored hair grew nearly to eyebrows that were so uncontrolled they made her look like a hairy young savage. George instructed the make-up department on how to remedy her faults and presently Rita Hayworth came through as that glittering sex symbol who entranced not only film fans but all of international society.

At the time George discovered Rita, she was in the process of getting rid of the first of many husbands; a nondescript character who was supposed to 'manage' her. I considered Rita a numb-skull until one day when she made the most endearing confession, 'Oh, Nita, I'm so dumb I'll always be making some terrible mistake!'

Just the same, Rita's marriage to Aly Khan was the greatest sex achievement since Cinderella landed Prince Charming. Aly was the quintessence of virility, intelligence, and charm. Raised in a culture where a gentleman must, perforce, be a womanizer, Aly handled his affairs with discretion. He was many cuts above suitors that Rita accepted later on.

Rita would ultimately have become the Begum Aly Khan, respected by her husband, revered by his entire nation; the richest wife in the world. Best of all, she could always have lived close to their enchanting daughter, the storybook Princess Yasmin. But Rita walked out on everything because

Harry Cohn summoned her back to his grubby old Hollywood studio to make a movie.

The smartest thing I ever knew Rita to do was when, in her youth, she told me how dumb she was.

Among the many story ideas that emanated from Hoppy's fertile brain was one that would team up Clark Gable with Mae West in a sex affair. As usual, Hoppy and I paced the Alley while we concocted our plot. Clark would be the star member of the Canadian Hockey Team known to the sports world as 'The Great Canadian.' Mae, through the demise of a sports-loving husband who owned the Canadians, would fall heiress to the team and its champion player. The two would first meet in the Widow's bedroom where, reclining on a chaise longue and dressed in a revealing negligee, the Widow languorously gave instructions to her team. The headstrong Canadian would resent being 'owned' by a female and their personalities would clash head-on. But at the same time our champion would have to fight off an ever-mounting sex urge. We told our plot to Irving who said enthusiastically, 'Why, it's a natural!'

But Mae West was under contract to Paramount and would have to be borrowed for the film. Her studio was more than anxious for her to appear with Gable, but left the decision up to Mae herself.

However, Mae, like Greta Garbo, was difficult to pin down. The main tenets of film-star psychology are to be mysterious, difficult, irrational, and suspicious, thus bringing about confusion and giving a star the whip hand. When Irving asked Mae for a conference at MGM, she refused. 'I never go off home base!' said Mae. Asked if she would listen to our story from one of its authors, namely me, Mae finally agreed and made a date to pick me up in front of the Beverly-Wilshire Hotel.

No fan could have been more excited than I, as I waited on the pavement for that creature who was already a legend. Hopefully, Mae would drive me off to her apartment where our conference would be held in her fabled white-and-gold drawing room, with its setup of trap drums on which Mae was said to be taking music lessons.

Presently a chocolate-colored Rolls-Royce town car pulled up in front of the Beverly-Wilshire with a handsome chocolate-colored chauffeur and footman, dressed in uniforms of the same color. The effect was a symphony in chocolate, except that Mae was decked in a cloud of white ostrich feathers.

Mae's ability to overpower any surroundings was incredible, for I found her to be as tiny as I, who couldn't have dominated an anthill. But a corset that pinched her waist pushed a smallish bosom upward and outward until it gave Mae a façade that the most buxom belle might envy.

'Get in, honey!' said Mae, 'and we'll hold our conference while we drive around Beverly Hills.' The reason for that ploy still baffles me. Perhaps Mae wanted to feel she could end our session at will by dumping me. So I was cheated out of a look at the mysterious hideaway that all Hollywood longed to see.

Driving about the streets of Beverly Hills I told Mae our plot. She was not impressed. And at a time when every other star in Hollywood would have made any sacrifice to play with Clark Gable, Mae turned him down.

She then explained her reason. 'Look, dear, I can't see myself horsing around with hockey players in a business way. It would make me feel unappealing. Any time I show my authority over the male sex it's got to be one-hundred-percent emotional. Your story line's okay, sweetheart, but take it from an old pro and cast that part with an MGM starlet named Roz Russell.'

But Irving refused Mae's hint to substitute Roz Russell for her so *The Great Canadian* will never be seen on any Late, Late TV show.

A time came when, much against my will, I was argued by producer Bernie Hyman into writing a movie far outside my own field. It concerned a distinguished lady in Texas who had made a career of rescuing illegitimate children and raising them in her own private orphanage. The Texas lady was widely quoted for her statement that 'There are no illegitimate children, there are only illegitimate parents.' And MGM paid her a large sum for that single line as basis for a movie to be titled *Blossoms in the Dust*.

It was a very tough assignment because there wasn't any plot. I went through weeks of the agony, frustration, trial-and-error that only an author can know. Several times I hit on a story line; followed it through with elation until, at the climax, the whole thing fell apart. At length I made an appointment to go to Bernie the next day and admit defeat. Dreading the encounter, I fell asleep nursing a grudge against Bernie for handing a gag writer like me such a hopeless assignment. But then, next morning, I woke up to find that a complete story line had been worked out by my subconscious mind during sleep.

It was based on the Texas lady's precept that even the most perfect orphanage creates traumas that can harm children for life; they should be gotten into real homes just as soon as possible.

With this as a premise, my story evolved around a crippled orphan whom the heroine undertook to cure and, during the process, developed a blind mother-love for the little boy. But with his cure, a day approached when she must hand him over for adoption. At which our heroine deviously found fault with the most ideal of foster parents. Then, in order to provide a normal home for the child, she decided to abandon the work of a lifetime; desert all the future orphans who might need her, in order to satisfy a possessive love for one single little boy. However, in a struggle with her conscience, our heroine's better nature won out. She released the child to a worthy young couple and continued the work to which she had dedicated her life.

When I kept my appointment with Bernie that morning, it was not to admit defeat but to tell him my soap-opera plot for which, as I recall, he kissed me.

In the making of a movie, emotionalism often used to spill off the sound stages onto the side lines. One day Bernie phoned me to hurry down to the set immediately. And there I walked into pandemonium.

Rehearsals had been in progress for the scene in which our Orphanage Lady and the little boy were to part forever. But the star who was playing the heroine objected violently to a certain line I'd written. In answer to an admonition not to cry, the small ex-cripple was to say, 'But I can cry *inside*, can't I?'

Now any child actor is a natural scene-stealer and it appeared that, during rehearsal, ours had caused even the cameramen and electricians to grow misty-eyed. So our star broke up the rehearsal to issue an ultimatum : unless that line was taken away from the little boy she would walk off the set. 'It's not in the psychology of a child to ask such a question,' she argued. 'On the other hand it would be quite in line for *me* to say "But you *can* cry inside, darling !"'

That small actor had run up against a more powerful scene-stealer than he was and the argument might have gone on endlessly while the studio clock ticked away at several thousand dollars a tick. So Bernie insisted we all repair to L. B.'s office for arbitration. And when the tough old autocrat heard that line, he himself dissolved into tears and ordered it to be kept where it belonged, in the mouth of the toddler.

As for me, the film that I had at first considered my Waterloo won me my first and only award of merit. And I hope it wiped out the derelictions of that *Red-Headed Woman* of mine.

19

Anatomy of a Part-Time Murderer

WHEN I was very young and first worked in Hollywood, the films had bred in me one sole ambition : to get away from them to live in the great world outside movies; to meet people who created their own situations through living them; who ad-libbed their own dialogue; whose jokes were not the contrivance of some gag writer.

But when I joined Irving Thalberg in 1931, he had turned all the inanity into excitement. He was like no other character in the entire film capital. While everybody else was bent on plugging his own personality, Irving remained aristocratically aloof. He never put his name on any of his films and he forbade its use by the publicity department. Irving worked for the pure love of creating. To share his precious anonymity was a rare privilege to a few of us like Hoppy and me. Our collaborations with him were, to me, almost like love affairs. They had many of the thrills, none of the drawbacks, and were certainly due to last longer.

The trouble was that option-time was drawing near and Mr E. was creating a series of terribly disturbing incidents. In order to make his presence felt by Irving, he'd interrupt our story conferences with suggestions that had no bearing on the matter at hand. So I'd speak up and clip Mr E. off. Afterward he'd ask, deeply hurt, 'Why do you never allow me. Our collaborations with him were, to me, almost like love been rude to him in public, but how else could I keep Mr

E. from interfering with work and causing Irving to drop our options?

Worst of all, those ocurrences were giving Mr E. a reason for wanting to murder his Buggie. One evening we were alone together in our living room when, without warning, he clutched my throat and started to choke me. He justified himself by the same type of argument that Scott Fitzgerald had pulled on Zelda and me, 'My little Bug is too good to live in a terrible world like this!' which wasn't much comfort. Mr E. was strong and wiry, while I weighed in at ninety pounds. Luckily our butler came into the room that time just as Scott's had done. Mr E. released me. Again was my life saved in the nick of time. George Jenkins was my good friend, as well as a good butler; I could always feel he kept an eye on me.

Mr E. lived in terror about his approaching option. I'd see a light in his bedroom in the middle of the night, tiptoe to his door, and look in. He'd be pacing the floor fully dressed, wringing his hands and muttering. 'Oh my God! What will become of me? I'm going to starve!' The question of starvation was egomania on Mr E.'s part, because his Bug, like anyone who made good with Irving, could easily find work at another studio.

At times David Selznick tried to lure me into that super-de-luxe corporation of his which was later responsible for *Gone with the Wind* and other movie classics. I would never have objected to David's work schedule because it was no more arduous than Irving's. But along with the labors of a Hercules, David, unlike Irving, had a total lack of consideration for his co-workers. Aldous Huxley once did a stint for him. 'That incredible man frequently phones me at three a.m. to say "My car is at your door. Get right over to the studio."'

But along with David's labors, he lived like a pasha. At

home he kept a triple staff of servants, so that his kitchen could function twenty-four hours a day for the numberless freeloaders that were his constant audience.

I had once had a taste of the heady atmosphere that hovered over David. As a weekend guest at his retreat on Bear Mountain, his brother Myron happened to mention a certain type of sausage he enjoyed at Maxim's in Paris. 'I'll order some for Sunday breakfast,' David spoke up casually. He forthwith got on the phone to his Paris representative, ordered him to put a supply of those sausages on a plane and have them flown directly to California. We ate them for breakfast on Sunday.

I would have been terribly unhappy to part from Irving, with whom luxury consisted in conjuring up ideas. There were times when Irving got requests from other studios to borrow me. He always refused, except on one occasion. Irving apologized when he announced he'd agreed to lend me to the Columbia studio. 'It's for a short job of writing dialogue,' Irving assured me, 'and they've offered to loan me Cary Grant in return.'

All Hollywood knew of the brutal tactics that made life a torment to those who worked for Harry Cohn at Columbia. So I reported there expecting the worst.

As a matter of fact, I got along very well with Cohn, personally; he had the engaging type of gangster wit that I respond to. But there were times that made me sick at heart when I had to witness his abuse of others. Today one needs only to read the incident of the molesting of a child actress in *The Godfather* for a description of the atrocities a few of those Hollywood producers might perpetrate.

I have forgotten everything about the job I did for Harry, except that I finished it in record time, escaped from the dank miasma that enveloped Columbia, and rushed home to the blessed comfort of Irving's office.

But later on an experience even more horrendous than my stint with Harry Cohn was to engulf me. I had gone to New York alone on a short holiday and in my absence an agent approached Mr E. with an offer from Sam Goldwyn. It was a deal that would equalize Mr E.'s salary with mine and the negotiations restored Mr E.'s spirits, placed him in the driver's seat, and made him feel tremendously important. On my return Mr E. met the train in a state of euphoria and told me he'd just signed a two-year agreement for us with Sam Goldwyn.

I was appalled. 'You mean that Irving let us go?' I gasped. At which Mr E. placed a finger parallel to his nose in a favorite gesture and winked craftily. 'I was too smart to deal with Irving! I went straight to Eddy Mannix!'

Mannix was the studio business manager and no great fan of Mr E.'s. So when told that we were discontented at MGM, Eddy forthwith canceled our contract.

Sam Goldwyn's reputation was only a notch above Harry Cohn's. But I didn't dare voice my dismay over what Mr E. had done for fear of plunging him into one of his terrifying depressions. At the same time, I couldn't keep from blurting out, 'What can I say to Irving? ... Or Hoppy?' 'Just trust your old boy, Buggie dear! You don't ever have to see them again. I've already moved your office equipment over to the Goldwyn Studio!'

When we reached home I was greeted by a mountain of red roses from Sam Goldwyn. But it didn't take away the grief of my parting from Irving, nor was it long before I learned that Sam had the quality which most strikes terror to my heart; he never knew what he liked. Our assignment was to write the script for a Western that would star Gary Cooper. I can't even remember its title now. But when I brought Sam a first outline, he beamed. 'Dot's beautifool. I adore your story line. Go ahead and write me a sample scene.' But a few days later when I read the scene to Sam he exploded, 'Dat story line stinks! Vot are you trying to do to me? Ruin Gary Cooper?'

It was a regular occurrence to be fired by Sam, but he always followed it with a fawning reinstatement, during which he might say 'I've just thought of an adorable vay for you to lick dot story!' He would then resurrect the very same story line that he'd recently tossed back into my teeth. So to be adored by Sam was even more heart-chilling than to have him chew me out.

If I was miserable at the Goldwyn studio, Mr E. was utterly devastated. Sam screamed at him even louder than at me; he once called Mr E. 'a dunce who lived by the sweat of his *Frau!*' And Mr E., realizing he'd jumped from the frying pan into a sizzling fire, sent me to Eddy Mannix to eat humble pie and ask if he'd take us back.

Mannix grinned when he remarked, 'I told Irving you couldn't take Sam for very long!' At any rate, he consented to reactivate our old contracts as soon as we could get out of our deal with Goldwyn. We had only to wait a day or two until Sam fired us again, and we took him up on it. Flabbergasted that anyone could resent his abuse, Sam was too stunned to utter – during which Mr E. said, 'Come along, Buggie!' and we quickly made an exit.

I must give Sam credit, however, that his system accomplished miracles. Once his films emerged from the snake pit of the Goldwyn studio, they were marvels of good taste. For Sam, in spite of his vulgarity, was a cultural snob and a great innovator. He brought George Balanchine to Hollywood, where the master created the first filmed sequences of pure ballet in *The Goldwyn Follies*. Sam imported Laurence Olivier from England when his genius had not yet been recognized at home. And I always marveled that a fine playwright like Bob Sherwood could create the Oscar-winning *The Best Years of Our Lives* for Goldwyn and still retain his sanity.

Bob once explained to me, 'One really can't resent Sam's vulgarity when he himself has never learned the meaning of the word. I find I can live with Sam just as one lives with high blood pressure.'

Then, too, there was always the comic relief of Sam's classic bloopers, such as his boast : 'I vant you to know that a Goldvyn comedy is not to be laughed at !'

But the greatest miracle Sam achieved was in the loyalty of his wife. Frances Goldwyn, born a lady and one of the great non-professional beauties of Hollywood, remained Sam's faithful helpmeet both at home and in his office through all their many years of marriage. Frances Goldwyn made me realize that one girl's poison could be another girl's champagne.

Well, my champagne was at MGM. But I'd returned only a little while before it supplied me with one more heady ache. Just before option time I was about to enter Mr E.'s office when I overheard Eddy Mannix cursing him out. I stopped to listen. It appeared that Mr E. had picked up some insignificant youngster outside the studio gate, promised her a film career, and then filmed an expensive test of her. 'Get this straight, Emerson !' I heard Mannix roar. 'The next time you pick up some little tramp, just pay her off yourself ! The studio isn't here to finance your sex life !'

How well I understood that poor Mr E.'s motivation had nothing to do with sex : he was trying to find *some* way to impress *anybody*. And not wanting to hear any more of Mannix's abuse, I stole quietly away, certain now that my days at MGM would soon be only a memory.

But the very next morning Irving summoned me to his office and announced that the studio wanted to extend my contract for five years but that Mr E.'s option would not be taken up. 'I can't justify wasting studio money by keeping John on the payroll,' said Irving.

There raced through my mind an awful vision of Mr E.'s

reaction to being let out. Among the nerve-racking incidents I'd lately gone through was one when George, our butler, had discovered a gun in Mr E.'s desk together with a bundle of suicide notes addressed to Irving, L. B., and several other executives. They were identical: 'Take care of my little Bug after I'm gone.'

In desperation, I came up with an alternative to Irving's offer. 'Would you mind splitting my salary in two, paying Mr E. half of it, and letting him stay on?'

While Irving gave me one of those long side glances of his, I added, 'I promise I'll keep him out of everybody's way.' 'All right, Nita,' Irving said, 'I'll agree to that. But you're a worse glutton for punishment than I've been.' I felt a very close bond with him at that moment.

20

Everything's All for the Best

AFTER my eighteen years at MGM were over, it became my
habit to spend summers at Montecatini, that Italian spa in
the Tuscan hills, forty-five minutes by motor from Florence.
Montecatini is a cure place but, seeing that I have no ailment, I go there because it is a restful spot.

The Hotel Pace is a fine example of Edwardian elegance
with a great deal of white marble from the neighboring
mountain of Carrara, from which Michelangelo got his
supply. I return there every year with the expectation
that the Pace will have been caught up in present-day
deterioration. But its old-world amenities and service still
exist, and its cuisine seems almost too delicious for cure
purposes.

During the mid-1950s, there were two summers when
my visits to the Pace were enriched by the presence of
Giovanni Papini, the Italian biographer and historian. His
Life of Christ had caused him to be excommunicated by the
Catholic Church, possibly because of the Signor's reverence
for actual fact. Signor Papini was in his mid-seventies, almost
blind, and suffering constant pain. An awareness that he
hadn't much longer to live never dimmed the Signor's
penetrating sense of humor. In many ways he reminded me of
Wilson Mizner. People who can laugh off misfortune as a
robust joke are pretty scarce.

Every day after lunch Signor Papini would be waiting for
me on the terrace of the Hotel Pace, bundled in shawls

although the weather was sunny and warm. It greatly amused him to listen to gossip about Hollywood.

Several years previously, Papini's *Life of Christ* had been bought by Warner Brothers and the Signor wondered why they never filmed it. There was a simple answer to that question : 'They never even *read* your book, Signor.' 'Then why did they pay such a large price for it?' 'Because it's easy for Jack Warner to sign a check, but to read a book is something else again.' The Signor understood and chuckled.

Signor Papini often took to dredging forth facts about my personal life. I had been a widow for several years and one day, spurred on by my old friend's curiosity, I described a certain shocking financial detail of my marriage and remarked that during the time Mr E. and I were under contract to MGM, I'd sometimes been puzzled when he instructed me, 'Buggie, I want you to tell everyone at the studio how much money I'm making on investments. Let people know that your salary is nothing in comparison with the vast sums that I make.' I promised but never carried out his instructions, knowing that folks weren't the least interested in my husband's financial prowess.

It was true that he was investing my salary at an unbelievably high rate of interest but, not understanding business, I never inquired into the subject.

There came a rather staggering explanation. An agent for a life-insurance company approached my brother and told him he ought to know that his brother-in-law was sinking all my money in annuities for his own, sole benefit. It then turned out that the nine-per-cent interest those annuities earned was due to Mr E.'s advanced age. But at his death, my money would all revert to the insurance company; I would be left without a penny.

'Mamma mia !' exclaimed Signor Papini.

'My brother was aghast too, Signor. He had always

indulged Mr E. as a rather harmless eccentric of whom he was rather fond. But to be stripping me of my money as fast as I made it, was going a bit too far!

'Clifford then began further investigations and learned that Mr E. had registered all my property in his own name; including the house for which my earnings had paid. Mr E. even got me to turn over to him the royalties on my books, without my being aware I'd signed them away.'

'I hope you put the rascal in jail,' Signor Papini declared.

'Well, Signor, my feelings about him were pretty complicated. When I first met Mr E., he had made use of my talent as nobody else had; not even D. W. Griffith. Then he directed my scripts for Douglas Fairbanks exactly as I wrote them; a tremendous satisfaction when most authors complain that Hollywood changes their work. Without his help, I might never have realized my potential or been encouraged to go on.'

'At the same time he was using you to further his own career,' interrupted Papini.

'That was beside the point, Signor. I adored Mr E. for years just as Galatea must have adored Pygmalion.

'Even my brother wanted to give Mr E. the benefit of an alibi. "I think the poor old codger's mind is affected," Clifford told me.

'Playing it cool, my brother inveigled Mr E. into seeing a specialist in mental disorders. Dr Shelton diagnosed the case almost on sight. It was only after years of consultations with *throat* specialists that we learned the true diagnosis of Mr E.'s strange behavior; his unmotivated optimism which alternated with despair; his cocksureness followed by dread of starvation; the affection for his Buggie that was coupled with attempts to kill her.'

'Your husband was a manic depressive?' asked Papini.

'Exactly, Signor. And, as a disease, it's very subtle in its progress. But now, when I read news of a suicide that is a "mystery," it's no mystery to me. I know the reason for it.

'Well, Signor, there's a sanatorium near the Santa Anita Race Track in Pasadena that's devoted to mental cases, alcoholism, and drug addictions. Because it is adjacent to Hollywood, its clientele is both wide and illustrious. During the years I went there to visit Mr E., I often encountered friends.

'Among them was W. C. Fields, bent on getting dried out when alcohol had made him soggy. He used to toddle into the premises accompanied by a ravishing Mexican girl he introduced as his "dietician." They occupied a bungalow where W. C. could adjust a garden hose so that it splattered against the windows and produced the sound of rain. I once found him turning on the faucet and muttering, 'This'll take the curse off that God-blasted California sunshine!' W. C. and I had a mutual longing for the New York rain, it was always a warm bond between us.

'The sanatorium used to be run by a Dr Smith whose wide experience made him more than a specialist; he was a humanitarian. He studied Mr E.'s case for a while and then asked me to come to Pasadena and see him privately, just as several of Mr E.'s doctors had done.

'"I know you're tremendously worried about your husband," Dr Smith said, "so I'd like to give you a briefing about his disease that will relieve your mind. But first of all I want you to take a look at his behavior unobserved. Come with me."

'The Doctor led me down a corridor to Mr E.'s door in which there was a small window of the type that allows one to see inside a room without being observed. Mr E. was pacing the floor, as he did so often, wringing his hands and muttering, "Oh, my God! Oh, my God!"

'Dr Smith ordered me to watch him closely. "Do you notice anything odd about his actions?"

'"No, I've often seen him like this. He's always the same."

'"Is that all you notice?"

'Mystified, I answered "Yes."

'"Look again and you'll see that he's constantly watching himself in the mirror."

'I looked and found it true; Mr E. was utterly fascinated by his image in the looking glass.

'"Your husband is enjoying every moment of a performance that would do credit to a Barrymore," said Dr Smith. "He's reveling in self-indulgence; a truly contented man."

'Dr Smith took me back to his office to explain further. "Manic depression is nothing more nor less than a monumental self-indulgence; a psychopathic egomania that gives no thought to anybody else and utterly disregards the grief it causes family and friends."

'When I asked the doctor about the possibility of a cure, he answered despairingly, "In all the years I've practiced, I've never found a cure for selfishness!"'

I related to Signor Papini a warning that Sherwood Anderson had given me quite early in my marriage. 'John has a psychopathic resentment of you!' Sherwood told me. 'He'll always belittle you, find mistakes in your work, put more and more commas into those manuscripts of yours. Take my warning for it, Nita, John might even try to kill you.'

I hadn't paid much attention to Swatty because I always considered that he was doused in gloom through trying to mimic Dostoevski and make us simple, uncomplicated Americans behave like Russian neurotics.

'But during Mr E.'s eighteen years of hospitalization, I witnessed all the nuances of manic depression; learned that nothing about the disease is rational. One day I heard news on the radio of the accidental death of Sherwood Anderson while on a tour of South America. He and Mr E. had been born in the same town of Clyde, Ohio, and all their lives had remained as close as brothers.

'Mr E. was then in a pleasantly manic state and I feared the death of our dear friend would plunge him into depression. I phoned his nurse and told her to hide the newspapers and keep Mr E. from listening to the radio.

'It worked! On Mr E.'s regular Sunday visit to Santa Monica he was most cheerful. But during lunch he interrupted a conversation to remark casually, "By the way, Buggie, I just heard that Swatty died down in South America."

'And on that awful afternoon when we sat around the radio listening to the broadcast of the Japanese bombing of Pearl Harbor, Mr E. assured us, "Pay no attention to it! It doesn't mean a thing!"

'Then would come episodes such as the one when I found Mr E. pacing the floor, wringing his hands and muttering, "I don't know what to do, Buggie! This morning at breakfast my teacup had a crack in it. I may be poisoned by germs. My God, what can I do?"

'At times when the manic phase took over, Mr E. became brilliant. During one such period he learned that the Los Angeles Symphony Orchestra was in dire straits. Mr E. had an idea for fund-raising. He moved into a Hollywood hotel, frenetically put his plan to work, guided it through to a satisfactory conclusion, and then slid into a depression that caused him to flee back to the waiting arms of Las Encinas.

'But Dr Smith assured me that if Mr E. had been an out-and-out scoundrel, he'd never have cracked up. He suffered acutely because of the harm he'd done. He used to weep and say, "If I should die, my Buggie will be left penniless; a beggar on the streets. What have I done to my little Bug?"

'But then, Signor, when my brother spent hours trying

to wheedle Mr E. to deed back to me the house my earnings paid for, Mr E. would whimper and plead, "Please don't hector me, Clifford! I'm a sick man!"' An argument that caused me to observe, 'In these days, Signor, anyone inclined to be a stinker can take a cue from old Dr Freud and call it a disease.' Patting my hand, Signor Papini said, 'Esatto!'

'Then sometimes, Signor, Mr E. would twist my arm and ask in terror "What's going to happen when I die, Buggie? Do you think God will forgive me?" "Of course," I would assure him. "But what evidence do you have there is a God? You're a smart girl. *Tell me!* What makes you so sure?"

' "Look, Mr E., I've simply got to worship any force that created Winston Churchill, Igor Stravinsky, George Balanchine, Joe E. Lewis, Duke Ellington, and the Marx Brothers – even if it's only spontaneous combustion." [N.B. I've just added Dr Kissinger to my list.] At any rate my arguments used to calm Mr E.

'At that, Mr E.'s life at Las Encinas was not devoid of a certain amount of fun. He would sometimes chase the comeliest nurses up and down the halls in the manner of Harpo Marx.'

'What a man!' said Signor Papini, and I could only agree.

'There came a rainy afternoon when Mr E. phoned Clifford in a frenzy. "Get over here to Pasadena right away! I'm at a massage parlor."

'Clifford knew what sort of massage parlor it was without having to be told.

'Well, Signor, my brother drove over to that massage parlor where a group of Pasadena oldsters were being held by police along with a staff of bleached blond "masseuses." Clutching Clifford's hand, Mr E. gasped, "Don't let Buggie hear about this. It would *kill* her!"

'Clifford told Mr E. to relax; used his influence with the

law, and got him sprung without having to report to the station along with the other sex culprits.

'After Clifford got Mr E. safely back to the sanatorium he called to tell me he'd just rescued my husband from being legally registered as a dirty old man. That we both laughed over Mr E.'s adventure would have killed *him*! Was I always to let that old boy down?

'I started to ruin my husband's life the very day I married him,' I told Signor Papini. 'I couldn't have done a better job if I'd been a blood-thirsty vampire played by Theda Bara.'

The Signor joined me in a chuckle and then turning pensive he asked, 'How long was your husband at that sanatorium?'

'Until the day he died; over eighteen years.'

'It must have cost you a fortune!'

'It never cost me a cent, Signor! Mr E. was kept by those annuities.'

The Signor, nodding in satisfaction, said, 'Bene! Bene!' And then he added, 'Better still, now you can make the scamp refund some of that money he stole.'

'But *how*, Signor?'

'Write him up and sell the story!'

... 'You're joking!'

'I'm serious, my dear! This is one of the instances that proves everything always turns out for the best in this worst of all possible worlds.'

21

Sex Can Make a Dunce of You

WHEN we children used to toddle forth to play on the cobble-stones of San Francisco, we only had to dodge trolley cars, horse-drawn vehicles, and bikes, since automobiles weren't yet in existence. Now we can watch a motor car as it ambles across the moon. The mores of our sex life have zoomed along just as dizzily, and whether they're forging ahead or in reverse might best be answered in terms of Hollywood.

In its heyday Hollywood reflected, if it did not actually produce, the sexual climate of our land. A screen love affair used to unfold chastely and without guile until it reached its climax in a kiss which, by a ruling of the Board of Censors, had quickly to fade out after seven seconds.

The lovers in those movies were products of the old American custom of men supporting women; so a girl's chief asset was the allure with which she disguised her normal acquisitiveness. That type reached its perfection in the gold diggers of the Twenties. Their technique might have been based on a theory that the most charming of all behavior lies in the canine species. Irving Thalberg used to tell me, 'When you write a love scene, think of your heroine as a little puppy dog, cuddling up to her master, wagging an imaginary tail, and gazing at him as if he were God.'

It would be heartening if men no longer craved that sort of treatment. But men are weak and constantly need reassurance, so now that they fail to find adulation in the opposite sex, they're turning to each other. And today, much as girls *look* like boys, they flunk out on the solicitude men are developing for each other. Less and less do men need women. More and more do gentlemen prefer gentlemen.

The Women's Lib movement seems unconcerned by this loss of manpower, but I'm not convinced they really are. Women's Libbers look so frustrated; their expressions are grim; and the two leaders who *are* pretty are rapidly losing their looks.

I am perfectly willing to accept the sneer of being a 'man-lover' with which Women Lib brands characters like me. I could even laugh off the theft of my money by a loved one, because I'd already conceded that sex was a great big cosmic joke. I had even stated that fact in a book, the heroines of which were a blonde who got no fun out of the game and a brunette who took pleasure in giving money to a man who resented her (as mine did).

In 1925 when H. L. Mencken read the manuscript of *Gentlemen Prefer Blondes*, he told me 'I'd publish this in the *American Mercury*, but I don't dare to affront my readers. Do you realize, young woman, that you're the first American writer ever to poke fun at sex?'

We've come quite a distance since then. Not long ago, a foremost American author was asked in a television interview, 'What is your feeling about sex, Mr Capote?' 'Well,' answered Truman, 'it's rather like a sneeze.'

I grant it can be powerful and sometimes impossible to smother; but one should still bear in mind that the aftermath of a sneeze may be nothing more than a damp Kleenex.

Not that falsified sex doesn't still have its protagonists. Norman Mailer, a less sturdy intellect than Capote, has written up his sensuous reactions to Marilyn Monroe in a book which reduces the literary 'he-man' into a latter-day Ella Wheeler Wilcox. But who can deny that the sort of permissiveness that Norman finds so 'sweet' can quickly be soured by unwelcome pregnancy, morning sickness, drugs, VD, divorce, and suicide.

George Bernard Shaw, a much more brilliant intellect than Mailer, was turned into a dunce when the erotic letters he wrote to Stella Campbell led to a humiliating cat-and-dog fight.

Sex, on the other hand, didn't fool the sophisticated writer Ludwig Bemelmans, who once complained to me about a shattered romance 'That affair was sheer ecstasy until sex entered in. Sex ruins everything !'

The farceur Goldoni, living in Venice during one of the world's most sensuous periods, gives sex a low rating, but wrote in pure rapture about the lifetime he shared with his wife, Nicolette. 'She has been my comfort in every moment. She knows just when I want her to leave me alone.'

Henrik Ibsen went on record to state, 'My eventual wife and I will live on separate floors, meet only at meal time, and address each other formally.' But then the poor dolt went on to make a marriage that landed him in a sexual morass.

Immanuel Kant stated his warning about sex by writing 'Philosophers don't marry.'

To go back to an even earlier day, 'The Song of Solomon' is the sexiest accolade ever written on that subject. But in his dotage Solomon collected 700 wives and 300 concubines and even Our Lord got fed up with him. 'Wherefore the Lord said "I will surely rend thy kingdom from thee !"'

Consider an incident that might have taken place between Our Lord and Satan. 'Look here,' the latter might have complained, 'you've gone ahead and created a whole universe and left me out of everything.'

'Very well, Satan, what do you want?'

'Just let me handle *sex*.'

The Lord agreed; Satan promptly brought about The Fall

and then inaugurated disasters of every sort: in a notable instance he only required one sexy blonde to instigate the Trojan War.

That our popular art forms have become so obsessed with sex has turned the U.S.A. into a nation of hobbledehoys; as if grown people don't have more vital concerns, such as taxes, inflation, dirty politics, earning a living, getting an education, or keeping out of jail.

It's true that the French have a certain obsession with sex, but it's a particularly adult obsession. France is the thriftiest of all nations; to a Frenchman sex provides the most economical way to have fun. The French are a logical race.

At this time, when pornography has become international legal tender, other countries are turning it out for profit. One worthy example was a Scandinavian movie titled *Without a Stitch*, in which the heroine happens to be a film actress. When required to perform a sex act on camera, she hesitates in deference to her family. 'Don't worry, my dear,' the director tells her, 'this movie will never be shown in Scandinavia; it's strictly for the American trade.'

Sex attraction, being entirely a matter of chance, has to be accepted where one finds it. Frequently, its victims have nothing else in common and the whole affair dwindles into a matter of chemistry. There's nothing colder than chemistry.

The few successful marriages I've known were between intellectuals who could regard a biological urge with fantasy; married pairs like Aldous and Maria Huxley, Edwin and Grace Hubble, Robert and Madeline Sherwood. Aside from intellectuals, I've known extremely successful marriages between joke-lovers, such as the two adorable Park Avenue clowns, Minnie and Herbie Weston.

During the 1920s we flappers patronized a beauty parlor where a lady barber used to shave certain hirsute areas into the shape of either a heart or a derby hat (the emblem of

Al Smith, a political idol of the day). Knowing Minnie Weston's love for jokes, I thought she'd have selected the design of Al's brown derby. She was shocked. 'Why, I couldn't be so unromantic! I chose the heart shape in honor of my Herbie!' Theirs was that most unique of all relationships: a sexy and happy marriage.

Most middle-class marriages in America are doomed, through lack of either the fantasy or sense of humor that can cope with their ever-recurrent challenges: the anxiety, discomfort, apprehension, and general messiness of sex.

After Bernard Shaw had learned the bitter truth about his liaison with Stella Campbell, he penned a résumé on the subject, stating in effect: 'I would like to detach ecstasy from indecency. Shakespeare wrote in a sonnet about "the expense of spirit in a waste of shame." Lord Chesterfield made that oft-quoted declaration that "the position is ridiculous, the pleasure momentary, and the expense damnable."

'Ideally, sex should have no reaction of disgust; no love-turned-to-hate. But there is a pleasure in thought – creative thought – that is entirely detached from ridiculous and disgusting acts and postures. My suggestion is that the passion of the body will ultimately become a passion of the mind!'

The old boy optimistically went on to declare that such an advent is possible to foresee. Man knew about flight long before he could fly, why can't the power that produced him fashion a better creature than Man, just as it did eons ago when the monkey proved not up to the mark?

G. B. S. went on to quote Browning:

Progress is
The law of life, Man is not man as yet.

In Shaw's masterwork, *Back to Methuselah*, he caused a learned Ancient to tell a young man, 'One moment of the ecstasy of life as I live it would strike you dead ... The day will come when there are no people but only thought. And that will be life eternal.'

The history of mankind, as we know it, has occupied no more than a split second in the Cosmic Scheme. So, give or take a few more eons, why can't human beings attain a state of weightless ecstasy?

A bumbling attempt was made to illustrate that situation in a disastrous musical, *Via Galactica*, in which a bodiless head existed for thought alone. The bumbling consisted in the dreariness of the old man's thoughts and the unfairness of giving him a young rival who was too well equipped from the waist down.

My own experience in sex turned a strong-willed character I had adored into a sick man. If only we'd remained sympathetic co-workers without the complication of marriage, no stranger would ever have addressed Mr E. as 'Mr Loos,' which made him try to strangle me.

The deepest and most enduring thrills of my lifetime were shared with men to whom I did *not* give in. In my romance with Viscount D'Abernon, his death intervened before we ever got together on that phony excuse of chasing down the paintings of Cranach the Elder.

Wilson Mizner and I had been kept apart by what I now realize to have been my heaven-sent impulse to play a practical joke. I admit that once in a while, thereafter, sex would rear its ugly head and Wilson would ask, 'What are we going to do about each other, Mama Nita?' The answer, thanks to our lucky stars, was 'Nothing.' Wilson was rapidly aging due to the wear-and-tear of dissipation; time would have been an invincible enemy, as it always has been, is now, and will forever be.

On a recent visit to Hollywood I discovered the extent to which sexuality has disappeared out there. Major studios which once harbored Mae West, Jean Harlow, and Cary

Grant have become tourist-traps where busloads of shoddy voyeurs gape at relics of the past, purchase hot dogs, soda pop, bubble gum, and souvenir snippets of film.

At the Beverly Hills Hotel, the Polo Room (named in honor of Darryl Zanuck's once favorite sport) still harbors a few stars, both male and female sporting the same surplus hair and slacks. They stride in like favorites of the Caesars in Alma-Tadema's noted painting but, now that movie productions is at its nadir, their attitude seems to be one of shameful boasting, 'Look at me! I've got a job!'

The Polo Room, however, is mostly a showcase for the hopeless, because the majority of superstars are hiding out in the Hollywood hills, racing along the freeways on their Hondas, or taking even more hair-raising trips on LSD.

In studying film production of the present day, I come upon a mystery, that many of those scabrous, not to say diabolic, movies do not pay back even the small sums required to outfit actors in the nude working in some rent-free shanty. Andy Warhol himself claims that the profits on his dirtiest film couldn't pay for a tiny diamond in the clasp of his idolized Paulette Goddard's necklace.

So now a chilling thought strikes me : are hard-core porno films secretly financed by our ideological enemies? Are they an element of psychological warfare in which innocent protagonists may not even realize that their youthful naughtiness is being used to destroy our moral fiber?

But whether this cynical thought is true or not, the forces of evil are now being challenged by a burgeoning cult among young people for Hollywood films. Teen-agers poisoned by the septic dandruff of *Hair*, or those who have copied the fashions of present day screen idols until they look like something left over from Halloween, will sit for half the night, glued to television screens, watching the pretty stars of those old movies on the Late, Late Show.

Young fry haunt the film theaters that specialize in ancient films. They crowd the projection room of the Museum of Modern Art. These kids spend their allowances on expensive picture albums that illustrate Hollywood's past. They are familiar with silent movie stars we oldsters have long since forgotten; they speak with warm nostalgia about Louise Glaum, Fay Tincher, and Slim Summerville. I am amazed when someone little more than a child informs me about an old cornball I wrote myself and have forgotten.

Recently at a gathering of the Association of Television Arts and Sciences a young writer asked me, 'Miss Loos, could I interview you on that silent film you wrote for Douglas Fairbanks called *The Mystery of the Leaping Fish?*' I could only apologize that I'd forgotten it completely. 'That may be a Freudian blackout,' she chuckled, 'It was a terrible flop.' 'Then why did you ever dig it up,' I asked. 'Because it's one of the few old films that hasn't yet been analyzed in the art magazines.'

Recently in Rochester, New York, I visited Eastman House, an institution dedicated to the history and art of the camera. It has a library of early movies which attracts students from all over the country. The auditorium, a fine example of Regency architecture, is superbly equipped. That afternoon I was ushered in to see Garbo's first American starring vehicle, *The Temptress*, filmed just before I arrived in Hollywood to do my eighteen-year stint on the MGM lot.

Students were watching *The Temptress* with reverence; several were making notes. Had I been doing likewise, I'm afraid they'd have recorded 'Roll eyes heavenward to demonstrate emotion,' 'Hand-on-the-hip indicates defiance!' In fact I didn't find anything about that old movie worth consideration; either its superheated plot or its technique. For my taste, *The Temptress*, Garbo, Antonio Moreno, *et al.*, belong in the trash can.

What is it that has sparked this obsession for vintage movies in a generation born long after they were released? I can only think that today's youth must subconsciously yearn for the very sentiments on which they've turned their backs. They must find a surcease for today's oafishness in the shimmering glamour of Jean Harlow, the angelic beauty of Lillian Gish, and the unchallenged masculine image of Clark Gable.

It's true that back in 1936, when Thalberg was preparing his script for *Camille*, he had progressed far beyond the crude technique of *The Temptress* and, by substituting passion with the gentle endearments of two young sweethearts, Irving attained the most profound catharsis of a love affair.

The same idyllic emotions used to be expressed in other popular art forms; today I recall a song of my youth that was imported from France. Its title was 'C'est si bon' meaning, of course, that love is 'so good.' But the ballad makers of today turn out lyrics which ask 'Is That All There Is?' That hard-bitten song, recorded by Peggy Lee, was bought by millions of young people, who apparently agreed with Peggy.

It's understandable that such defeatism has resulted in impotence; that composers now write such lyrics as 'We almost made it, didn't we, girl?' *Almost!* What kind of a situation is *that* to celebrate in song?

Another ballad tells of a swain who is on his way to Phoenix in order to *get away* from his sweetheart. Yet another makes no mention of love, pro or con, but glorifies an ability to disregard raindrops that keep falling on his head.

All these ditties make me long to hear Eddie Cantor once again, jumping up and down in delight, clapping his little white-gloved hands and exclaiming 'If You Knew Susie Like I Know Susie!'

I also regret the cheek-to-cheek dancing which has been

replaced by wide spaces between partners. Each one dances *alone*. I remember the camaraderie we used to achieve on bathtub gin; whereas today's kids, stoned on pot, retire inside their own personalities. They may be happy, but they seldom laugh.

In time, decrepitude will overtake me and I myself may lose the capacity to laugh. This is a likelihood which once inspired the British poet William Empson to pen:

REFLECTION FROM ANITA LOOS

No man is sure he does not need to climb,
It is not human to feel safely placed.
'A girl can't go on laughing all the time.'

Love rules the world but is it rude, or slime?
All nasty things are sure to be disgraced.
A girl can't go on laughing all the time.

It is too weak to speak of rights and crime
Gentlemen prefer bound feet and the wasp waist.
A girl can't go on laughing all the time.

It gives a million gambits for a mime
On which a social system can be based:
No man is sure he does not need to climb,
A girl can't go on laughing all the time.

That poem confuses me; either it doesn't quite make sense or I'm fearful that, with study, Empson will make too much sense and at this late age I'll suddenly turn into a weeper.

But I have no intention of dramatizing my feelings about Hollywood. In the past, as now, it was a stamping ground for tastelessness, violence, and hyperbole, but once upon a time it turned out a product which sweetened the flavor of life all over the world.

And it would now appear that the spirit of those old films is rising from the dust to assure a new generation that the permissiveness of the 1970s is a killjoy; that those gyrations of naked bodies which once would have made the Board of Censors reach for its scissors, lead to nothing.

And if we have to tell Hollywood good-by, it may be with one of those tender, old-fashioned, seven-second kisses exchanged between two people of the *opposite* sex, with all their clothes on.

Screenplays by Anita Loos

HEADNOTE: Included here is a list of Miss Loos's screenplays, and all available information about them. After the title appears, in order, the length of the film, the amount she was paid for it, the type of film, the director, and members of the cast whenever possible. The films are listed by production company, according to the year they were sold.

1912
Films Sold and Released
American Biograph
    The Road to Plaindale. 1 reel. $25. Released in 1914.
    The Power of the Camera. ½ reel. $15. Released in 1913.
    The New York Hat. 1 reel. $25. Released in 1913. D. W. Griffith.
    Miss Loos's third sale and said to be her first film. With Mary Pickford, Lionel Barrymore, and Lillian and Dorothy Gish.
Films sold (never produced)
American Biograph
    He Was a College Boy. ½ reel. $15.
Lubin
    The Earl and the Tomboy. 1 reel. $25.

1913
Films Sold and Released
American Biograph
    A Horse on Bill. ½ reel. $15.
    A Hicksville Epicure. ½ reel. $15.
    Highbrow Love. ½ reel. $15.
    A Hicksville Romance. ½ reel. $25.

A *Fallen Hero*. ½ reel. $25.

A *Fireman's Love*. ½ reel. $25. With Fay Tincher.

A *Cure for Suffragettes*. ½ reel. $25.

The Suicide Pact. ½ reel. $25.

Binks Runs Away. ½ reel. $25.

How the Day Was Saved. ½ reel. $25.

When a Woman Guides. 1 reel. $35.

Fall of Hicksville's Finest. ½ reel. $25.

The Wedding Gown. 1 reel. $25.

Yiddish Love. ½ reel. $25.

Gentlemen and Thieves. 1 reel. $30.

A *Bunch of Flowers*. 1 reel. $35. Drama.

Pa Says. Dell Henderson. With Ed Dillon and Dorothy Gish.

The Widow's Kids. With Dorothy Gish.

The Lady in Black. With Ed Dillon, Dorothy Gish, and Gertrude Bambrick.

Reliance Mutual

The Deacon's Whiskers. $50. Farce. With Fay Tincher.

His Awful Vengeance. $50. Farce.

All for Mabel. $50. Farce.

The Fatal Deception. $25. Farce.

For Her Father's Sins. 1 reel. $50. With Blanche Sweet.

Kornick

Unlucky Jim. 1 reel. $35.

All on Account of a Cold. 1 reel. $25.

Cinemacolor

The Saving Grace. 1 reel. $25.

A *Narrow Escape*. 1 reel. $25.

Two Women. 1 reel. $25.

Lubin

The Wall Flower. 1 reel. $25.

Films Sold (never produced)

American Biograph

Queen of the Carnival. ½ reel. $25.

The Mayor Elect. ½ reel. $25.

The Making of a Masher. ½ reel. $25.

Path of True Love. ½ reel. $25.
A Girl Like Mother. ½ reel. $25.
The Mother. 1 reel. $35.
The Great Motor Race. ½ reel. $25. Farce.
His Hoodoo.

1914
Films Sold and Released
American Biograph
   The Meal Ticket. $25. Drama.
   The Saving Presence. $35. Drama.
   The Suffering of Susan. $25. Comedy.
Reliance Mutual
   The Chieftain's Daughter (Some Bull's Daughter). $25. Farce.
   The Fatal Dress Suit. $50. Farce.
   The Girl in the Shack. 1 reel. $75. Drama.
   The Saving Presence. $35. Drama.
   His Hated Rival. $50. Farce. With Chester Conklin.
   A Corner in Hats.
   Nearly a Burglar's Bride. $50. Farce. With Fay Tincher.
   The Fatal Curve (Izzy and His Rival).
   The Million-Dollar Bride. $50. Farce.
   A Flurry in Art. $50. Comedy melodrama.
   Nellie, the Female Villain. $50. Farce. With Fay Tincher.
American
   His Rival. $25. Comedy drama.
   Where the Roads Part. $25. Drama.
Films Sold (never produced)
American Biograph
   A No Bull Spy. $25.
   A Balked Heredity. $25. Drama.
   A Blasted Romance. $25. Farce.
   Mortimer's Millions. $25. Comedy.
   A Life and Death Affair. $25. Farce.
   The Sensible Girl. $35. Drama.
   At the Tunnel's End. $35. Melodrama.

Reliance Mutual
   The Deadly Glass of Beer. $25. Farce.
   The Stolen Masterpiece. $50. Farce.
   The Last Drink of Whiskey. $25. Farce.
   Nell's Eugenic Wedding. $25. Farce.
   The School of Acting. $50. Farce.
   A Hicksville Reformer. $50. Farce.
   The White Slave Catchers. $25. Farce.
   The Style Accustomed. $25. Farce.
   The Deceiver. $50. Farce.
   How They Met. $50. Comedy melodrama.

1915
Films Sold and Released
American Biograph
   The Cost of a Bargain. $35. Drama.
Reliance Mutual
   Sympathy Sal. $75. Drama.
   Nelly, the Female Victim. $50. Farce. With Fay Tincher.
   Mixed Values. $50. Comedy. With Fay Tincher.
Metro
   Pennington's Choice. From a story by J. A. Culley. O. A.
   Lund With Francis X. Bushman, Beverly Bayne. (*A Girl Like I*
   states $500 for script; the Museum of Modern Art list states
   $100.)
Films Sold (never produced)
American Biograph
   The Tear on the Page. $50. Drama.
   How to Keep a Husband. Comedy.
Reliance Mutual
   The Burlesquers. $50. Farce.
   The Fatal Fourth. $50. Farce.
   The Fatal Fingerprints. $35. Comedy.
   Wards of Fate. $40. Drama.
Pictorial Review
   Heart that Truly Loved. $150.

Fine Arts
The Little Liar. $500. With Mae Marsh.
Mabel Normand (produced the film)
Mountain Bred. $200.

1916
Films Sold and Released
Macbeth. Titles arranged by Anita Loos. John Emerson (director).
With Sir Herbert Beerbohm-Tree.
Metro
A Corner in Cotton. $200. Fred J. Balshofer. With Margaret Snow.
Triangle-Fine Arts
Wild Girl of the Sierras. $100. Collaboration with F. M. Pierson. Paul Powell. With Mae Marsh and Robert Harron.
Calico Vampire. $200. With Fay Tincher.
Laundry Liz. $200. With Fay Tincher.
French Milliner. $200. With Fay Tincher.
The Wharf Rat. $250. Chester Withey. With Mae Marsh and Robert Harron.
Stranded. $300. Lloyd Ingraham. With DeWolf Hopper.
The Social Secretary. John Emerson. With Norma Talmadge, Gladden James, Kate Lester, Erich von Stroheim, Helen Weir, Herbert French, and Vivian Ogden.
His Picture in the Papers. $500. John Emerson. With Douglas Fairbanks.
The Half-Breed. From 'In the Carquinez Woods,' by Bret Harte. Allan Dwan. With Douglas Fairbanks.
American Aristocracy. $500. Lloyd Ingraham. With Douglas Fairbanks, Charles de Lima, Jewel Carmen, and Albert Parker.
Manhattan Madness. Allan Dwan. With Douglas Fairbanks, Jewel Carmen, George Beranger, Ruth Darling, and Marcey Harlan.
The Matrimaniac. Collaboration with John Emerson from a

story by Octavus Roy Cohen and J. V. Glesy. Paul Powell. With Douglas Fairbanks and Constance Talmadge.

Wark

Intolerance. Screenplay by Frank Woods. Written, directed, and produced by D. W. Griffith. Cameraman – G. W. (Billy) Bitzer. Titles – Anita Loos. With Mae Marsh, Robert Harron, and Fred Turner.

1917

Films Sold and Released

Triangle-Fine Arts

The Americano. Based on the story, 'Blaze Derringer,' by Anita Loos. John Emerson. With Douglas Fairbanks, Alma Rubens, and Lote du Crote.

Douglas Fairbanks Film Corporation

In Again, Out Again. Photographed by Victor Fleming. With Douglas Fairbanks, Arline Pretty, Walter Walker, Arnold Lucy, and Homer Hunt.

Wild and Wooly. Based on a story by H. B. Carpenter. John Emerson. Photographed by Victor Fleming. With Douglas Fairbanks and Eileen Percy.

Reaching for the Moon. Collaboration with John Emerson. John Emerson (director). Photographed by Victor Fleming and Sam Lardners. Art Director – Wilfred Buckland. With Douglas Fairbanks, Richard Cummings, and Eileen Percy.

Down to Earth. Based on a story by Douglas Fairbanks. John Emerson. With Douglas Fairbanks and Eileen Percy.

1918

Films Sold and Released

Paramount

Let's Get a Divorce. Collaboration with John Emerson. From Divorçons, a play by Victorien Sardou. Charles Giblyn. With Billie Burke. Reviewed in the New York Times 4/29/18.

Come On In. Collaboration with John Emerson. John Emerson.

With Shirley Mason and Ernest Truex. Reviewed in the *New York Times* 9/23/18.

Goodbye Bill. Collaboration with John Emerson. John Emerson. With Shirley Mason and Ernest Truex.

Art

Hit-the-Trail Holiday. Collaboration with John Emerson. From the play of the same name by George M. Cohan. Marshall Neilan.

1919

Films Sold and Released

Paramount

Oh, You Women! Collaboration with John Emerson. Based on a story by Anita Loos and John Emerson. John Emerson. With Ernest Truex and Louis Huff.

Cosmopolitan Select

Getting Mary Married. In collaboration with John Emerson. Allan Dwan. With Marion Davies, Norman Kerry, and Frederick Burton.

First National

A Temperamental Wife. In collaboration with John Emerson. David Kirkland. With Constance Talmadge, Wyndham Standing, and Ben Hendricks. Reviewed in the *New York Times* 9/15/19.

Virtuous Vamp. In collaboration with John Emerson. From *The Bachelor*, a play by Clyde Fitch. David Kirkland. With Constance Talmadge, Jack Kane, and Conway Tearle. Reviewed in the *New York Times* 11/17/19.

Selznick

The Isles of Conquest. In collaboration with John Emerson. From *By Right of Conquest*, a novel by Arthur Hornblow. Edward Jose. With Norma Talmadge, Natalie Talmadge, and Wyndham Standing. Reviewed in the *New York Times* 10/27/19.

1920

Films Sold and Released
First National

Two Weeks. In collaboration with John Emerson. From At the Barn, a play by Anthony Wharton. Sidney Franklin. With Constance Talmadge.

In Search of a Sinner. In collaboration with John Emerson. David Kirkland. With Constance Talmadge and Radcliffe Fellows. Reviewed in the New York Times 3/8/20.

The Love Expert. In collaboration with John Emerson. David Kirkland. With Constance Talmadge.

The Perfect Woman. In collaboration with John Emerson. David Kirkland. With Constance Talmadge.

The Branded Woman. In collaboration with John Emerson. From the play by Oliver D. Bailey. Albert Parker. With Norma Talmadge.

1921

Films Sold and Released
First National

Dangerous Business. In collaboration with John Emerson. R. William Neill. With Constance Talmadge.

Mama's Affair. In collaboration with John Emerson. From the play by Rachel Barton Butler. Victor Fleming. With Constance Talmadge.
Reviewed in the New York Times 1/24/21.

A Woman's Place. In collaboration with John Emerson. Victor Fleming. With Constance Talmadge.

1922

Films Sold and Released
First National

Red Hot Romance. In collaboration with John Emerson. Victor Fleming. With Basil Sydney and Mary Collins. Reviewed in the New York Times 1/23/22.

Polly of the Follies. In collaboration with John Emerson. With Joseph Plunkett and Constance Talmadge.

1923
Film Sold and Released
First National
   Dulcy. In collaboration with John Emerson. From a play by
   George S. Kaufman and Marc Connelly. Sidney Franklin. With
   Constance Talmadge.

1924
Film Sold and Released
Associated Exhibitors
   Three Miles Out. In collaboration with John Emerson. From
   a story by Neysa McMein. Irvin Willat. With Madge Kennedy.

1925
Film Sold and Released
First National
   Learning to Love. In collaboration with John Emerson. Sidney
   Franklin. With Constance Talmadge and Antonio Moreno.
   Reviewed in the *New York Times* 2/23/25.

1928
Film Sold and Released
Paramount
   Gentlemen Prefer Blondes. In collaboration with John Emer-
   son. From the novel by Anita Loos. Malcolm St Clair. With
   Ruth Taylor, Alice White, Emily Fitzroy, Mack Swain, Ford
   Sterling, Holmes Herbert, and Trixie Friganza. Reviewed by the
   New York Times 1/16/28.

1932
Films Sold and Released
MGM
   Red-Headed Woman. From the novel by Katharine Brush.
   Jack Conway. With Jean Harlow, Chester Morris, and Lewis
   Stone.
   Blondie of the Follies. Original story by Frances Marion with

dialogue by Anita Loos. Edmund Goulding. With Marion
Davies and Robert Montgomery.

1933
Films Sold and Released
MGM

Hold Your Man. In collaboration with Howard Emmett Rogers.
Music and lyrics by Nacio Herb Brown and Arthur Freed.
From a story by Anita Loos. Sam Wood. With Jean Harlow,
Clark Gable, and Stuart Erwin. Reviewed by the *New York
Times* 7/1/33.
The Barbarian. In collaboration with Elmer Harris. From a
story by Edgar Selwyn. Sam Wood. With Ramon Novarro and
Myrna Loy.

1934
Films Sold and Released
Columbia

Social Register. Screenplay by Clara Beranger, James Ashmore
Creelman, and Grace Perkins. From the play by John Emerson
and Anita Loos. Marshall Neilan. With Colleen Moore.
MGM

The Girl from Missouri. In collaboration with John Emerson.
Jack Conway. With Jean Harlow, Lionel Barrymore, and
Franchot Tone. Reviewed by the *New York Times* 8/4/34.
Biography of a Bachelor Girl. From the stage play *Biography*
by S. N. Behrman. Edward H. Griffith. Photographed by
James Wong Howe. With Ann Harding and Robert Mont-
gomery. Reviewed by the *New York Times* 3/2/35.

1935
Film Sold and Released
MGM

Riffraff. In collaboration with Frances Marion and H. W. Hane-
man. From a story by Frances Marion. J. Walter Ruben. With
Jean Harlow, Spencer Tracy, and Una Merkel. Reviewed by the
New York Times 1/13/36.

1936
Film Sold and Released
MGM

San Francisco. From a story by Robert Hopkins. Score by Herbert Stotheart. W. S. Van Dyke II. Produced by John Emerson and Bernard H. Hyman. With Clark Gable, Jeanette MacDonald, Spencer Tracy, and Jack Holt. Reviewed in the *New York Times* 6/27/36.

1937
Films Sold and Released
MGM

Mama Steps Out. George B. Seitz. With Guy Kibbee, and Alice Brady.

Saratoga. In collaboration with Robert Hopkins. Score by Edward Ward. Songs by Walter Donaldson, Bob Wright, and Chet Forrest. Jack Conway. With Clark Gable, Jean Harlow, and Lionel Barrymore. Produced by Bernard H. Hyman. Reviewed by the *New York Times* 7/23/37.

1938
Films Sold (never produced)
MGM

The Great Canadian.
Alaska.

1939
Film Sold and Released
MGM

The Women. In collaboration with Jane Murfin. From the play by Clare Boothe. George Cukor. Produced by Hunt Stromberg. With Norma Shearer, Joan Crawford, Rosalind Russell, Mary Boland, and Paulette Goddard. Reviewed by the *New York Times* 9/22/39.

1940

Film Sold and Released

MGM

Susan and God. From a play by Rachel Crothers. George Cukor. Produced by Hunt Stromberg. With Joan Crawford, Fredric March, and Ruth Hussey. Reviewed in the *New York Times* 7/12/40.

1941

Films Sold and Released

MGM

They Met in Bombay. Collaboration with Edwin Justus Mayer and Leon Gordon from a story by Franz Kafka. Clarence Brown. With Clark Gable, Rosalind Russell, and Peter Lorre. Reviewed by the *New York Times* 7/4/41.

When Ladies Meet. In collaboration with S. K. Lauren. From a play by Rachel Crothers. Robert Z. Leonard. Produced by Robert Z. Leonard and Orville O. Dull. With Joan Crawford, Robert Taylor, and Greer Garson. Reviewed by the *New York Times* 9/5/41.

Blossoms in the Dust. From a story by Ralph Wheelwright. Mervyn LeRoy. Produced by Irving Asher. Filmed in Technicolor. With Greer Garson, Walter Pidgeon, and Felix Bressart. Reviewed in the *New York Times* 6/27/41.

1942

Film Sold and Released

MGM

I Married an Angel. From the musical play by Vaszary Janos, Lorenz Hart, and Richard Rodgers. W. S. Van Dyke II. Produced by Hunt Stromberg. With Jeanette MacDonald, Nelson Eddy, and Edward Everett Horton. Reviewed by the *New York Times* 7/10/42.

1953
Film Sold and Released
20th Century-Fox
   Gentlemen Prefer Blondes. By Charles Lederer based on musical
comedy by Anita Loos in collaboration with Joseph Fields.
Produced by Sol C. Siegel. Music by Jule Styne. Lyrics by Leo
Robin. New songs by Hoagy Carmichael and Harold Adamson.
Dances by Jack Cole. Howard Hawks. With Jane Russell,
Marilyn Monroe, Charles Coburn, Elliot Reid, Tommy Noonan,
George Winslow, Marcel Dalio, and Taylor Holmes. Reviewed
in the *New York Times* 7/16/53.

The book for *Lorelei*, a musical based on the musical comedy
Gentlemen Prefer Blondes, was also by Anita Loos and Joseph
Fields, revised by Kenny Solms and Gail Parent; the score was
by Jule Styne and Leo Robin, with new lyrics by Betty Comden
and Adolph Green.

MORE ABOUT PENGUINS
AND PELICANS

Penguinews, which appears every month, contains details of all the new books issued by Penguins as they are published. From time to time it is supplemented by our stocklist which includes around 5,000 titles.

A specimen copy of *Penguinews* will be sent to you free on request. Please write to Dept EP, Penguin Books Ltd, Harmondsworth, Middlesex, for your copy.

In the U.S.A.: For a complete list of books available from Penguins in the United States write to Dept CS, Penguin Books, 625 Madison Avenue, New York, New York 10022.

In Canada: For a complete list of books available from Penguins in Canada write to Penguin Books Canada Ltd, 2801 John Street, Markham, Ontario LR3 1B4.

Some other Penguins of interest:

ZELDA FITZGERALD
Nancy Milford

'I don't want you to see me growing old and ugly ... we will just *have* to die when we're thirty – Zelda in 1919

As the radiant muse who inspired and haunted Fitzgerald's fiction, Zelda Sayre is immortalized. But her words were cruelly prophetic – for by the time they were forty the legendary Fitzgeralds had crashed on the rocks of drink and insanity.

Nancy Milford's thoughtful, sympathetic biography traces the transition of a wild Southern belle into a tragic, half-mad woman who died in a hospital fire.

THE NOWHERE CITY
Alison Lurie

Alison Lurie holds up life in Los Angeles for her ruthless inspection.

'Very rarely does one come across a novel so well constructed that it surges with life on all levels. It is a remarkably penetrating story of a city without an identity' – *Daily Telegraph*

'A very witty, assured, sustained creation of both people and place' – *New Statesman*

SLOUCHING TOWARDS BETHLEHEM
Joan Didion

Joan Didion, as always acerbic, reflective, humorous, knowledgeable, and unfailingly honest, delivers her verdicts on The Great American Way of Life.

Her title essay, describing the hippies of San Francisco, reflects her main theme – 'that things fall apart'. And, among other subjects, she reports on Joan Baez, looks wryly at John Wayne, airs her views on morality, analyses California and Hawaii, and pauses for a searching backward glance into her youth.

INDIA: A WOUNDED CIVILIZATION
V. S. Naipaul

'This is a stern attempt to break through the understandable yet entirely disabling sentimentality with which India is invariably viewed. Much less diverting than the earlier memoir *An Area of Darkness*, and intentionally so; but much more worrying' – Martin Amis in the *Observer*

India: A Wounded Civilization challenges so many cliches that it is bound to raise protest, but it is a book written out of love and with the creative sympathy of a great novelist.

WORDPOWER:
AN ILLUSTRATED DICTIONARY OF VITAL WORDS
Edward de Bono

'Wordpower is to the mind what horsepower is to the car.' The 265 specialized words that Dr de Bono defines here are most of them familiar, at least in part; some, because of their usefulness, are borrowed from scientific, technical and business fields. All are powerful tools of expression if used precisely. Here they are defined in terms of usage and with the help of cartoons and illustrations to enable the reader to adopt them into his everyday vocabulary. The wordpower they offer make a dynamic addition to anyone's education.

BIKO
Donald Woods

This book is at once a powerful biographical sketch of the young South African leader Steve Biko, and a flaming indictment of the South African Government. Donald Woods, the outspoken editor of the *East London Daily Despatch*, escaped from South Africa in 1977 and is already established as an eloquent and informed commentator on South African affairs. His *Biko* recounts the arrest and the violent death in custody of this remarkable young politician. It makes harrowing reading.

MOKSHA

Aldous Huxley

Moksha, liberation, Nirvana, a trip: expressions differ, but the human yearning to transcend the limitations of the physical self is universal – the desire to take, in Aldous Huxley's words, a 'holiday from reality'.

In these collected writings on this eternally stimulating theme, the creator of *Brave New World* explores the brave new dawn of the psychedelic mind-changing drugs, mescalin and LSD. With the lucid appraisal of the philosopher, the reverent curiosity of the mystic and the clinical detachment of the scientist, he discusses their political, medical and ethical implications: and with the eloquence of the poet and the power of the visionary, he describes his own experience of them, in the fullness of life and in the hour of his death.

THE PLEASURE GARDEN

Anne Scott-James and Osbert Lancaster

From Roman peristyle to 20th-century patio, Anne Scott-James conducts us through 2000 years of the English garden; to linger, first in simple, enclosed courtyards of medieval days and the formal showpieces of Jacobean England, and later, to wander through sweeping, moody landscapes of the 18th century. We learn of each age's distinguished botanists, designers and architects, who employed the social conditions and the fads and fashions of the time to shape the gardens of their day.

Anne Scott-James's witty and informative text and Osbert Lancaster's delightful drawings are so evocative that we can almost smell the flowers as we step from one bower of pleasure to another.